DAVID MEYL

WHEN
TIGERS
ROARED

AN AUTOBIOGRAPHY
WITH FINTAN O'TOOLE

PUBLISHED BY HERO BOOKS
1 WOODVILLE GREEN
LUCAN
CO. DUBLIN
IRELAND

Hero Books is an imprint of Umbrella Publishing
First Published 2022
Copyright © David Meyler and Fintan O'Toole

A CIP record for this book is available from the British Library

ISBN 9781910827604

Cover design and formatting: jessica@viitaladesign.com
Photographs: Dave Lofthouse, Inpho and The Meyler Family Collection

DEDICATION

To
Cally, Alanna and Brody

CONTENTS

ACKNOWLEDGEMENTS

I WISH TO thank my wife Cally, the most important person in my life… my friend and mother of our treasured children Alanna and Brody.

To my parents John and Stella, for their love and support over the years, and to my sister Sarah for her advice and help, always. To Cally's parents Jimmy and Ann, who have helped so much through our life together.

I wish to acknowledge the support of all my schools – Beaumont NS, St Anthony's NS Ballinlough, CBC, and Bruce College, a big thank you for my education. And to Blackrock National Hurling Club and St Michael's Football Club, thank you for developing me as a young lad and preparing me for the hard knocks in later life.

To College Corinthians AFC where I started as a six-year-old… treasured memories and friendships. To Cobh Ramblers FC and Cork City FC for maturing me and preparing me for the road ahead in England.

A special thanks to all the coaches and managers throughout my career. To Roy Keane, Neil Bailey, Steve Bruce and Martin O Neill for continuing my development, and to the wonderful supporters of the Red and White. To Hull City AFC for taking me on board in 2012 and a heartfelt thanks to the Allam family, to Steve Bruce once again, Mike Phelan, Marco Silva, Leonid Slutsky and Nigel Adkins for their continued support, and to all the supporters of Hull City AFC. A massive thanks for our incredible years together in the Premiership and Europe, and our never to be forgotten FA Cup journey. My gratitude to each and every one of you.

Thank you to Reading FC, and Coventry City FC and Mark Robins, for my last few years as a professional footballer.

Finally to Ireland! My deepest sense of gratitude and appreciation for allowing me fulfil my boyhood dreams of playing and captaining my country, the greatest honour you can achieve. To my Ireland teammates, and to my Ireland managers, especially Martin and Roy. To all the Irish supporters… the Boys in Green. A massive thank you to you all.

David Meyler
August 2022

PROLOGUE

Birmingham
January 5, 2011

I'M LYING ON a physio bed that has been set up in the showers of the away dressing-room at Villa Park. My dad is on one side of me. Sunderland manager Steve Bruce is on the other.

I'm crying.

Steve has tears in his eyes; dad is welling up as well. It's Wednesday night football in the Premier League.

My right knee is the problem, just like it was last May when I first tore my cruciate… like it will be in the future.

IT WAS MY first time playing against Aston Villa, the club I was on trial with as a teenager.

From the kick-off, I was eager to get going in midfield. Midway through the first-half the ball bounced and came toward Carlos Cuéllar, the Villa defender. He shaped to pass the ball… and I ran in, raising my leg to block it off. Carlos dummied and moved the opposite way.

I reacted and tried to push off in that direction. But I made that split-second decision when my leg was in the air, my body already moving off and… when my knee landed… it wobbled.

I fell to the ground.

A LOT OF people said I'd rushed back; my knee wasn't strong enough and my recovery hadn't been right. I know none of those were a factor. It was just a freak moment.

It could have happened walking down a stairs… you're not paying attention, you misjudge the step… you could land and buckle your knee.

I was stretchered off and brought down the stadium tunnel by the medical staff. Dad had come down from his seat in the stand – I could hear him shouting with the security to let him into the dressing-room. They were not for budging, and it took a Sunderland official to step in to wave him through.

He came in to me, and by half-time Steve has joined him.

THERE'S A CONSTANT queue of Sunderland players, checking to see how I am. There's a lot of emotion in the air; I can see people are hurting for me.

It's 248 days since I destroyed my knee the first time, when we played Manchester United at the Stadium of Light. It's only 25 days since I made my comeback against Fulham at Craven Cottage.

It's 0-0 against Villa. The boss is trying to get the team going as they go out for the second-half.

Steve turns and points at me… 'Go and win it for him!'

The team does just that; Phil Bardsley scores the winner with 10 minutes left. Emile Heskey is sent-off in the second-half for Villa and their manager Gerard Houllier is under big pressure.

Villa have slipped into the relegation places.

It's a good win for us, but three points can't lift my spirits.

CHRISTMAS HAD BEEN good. My family all came over from Ireland. On December 26, I realised an ambition that my nan had long held; that her grandson would get to play at Old Trafford, the home of the club she supported.

On New Year's Day, I played the full 90 minutes as we beat Blackburn 3-0. It was a perfect home performance, the Sunderland fans were full of life. Danny Welbeck and Darren Bent scored early on, Asamoah Gyan came off the bench to get the third.

We climbed to seventh. It was a brilliant Saturday afternoon and then we were heading to play Aston Villa full of energy.

A COUPLE OF nights before that game, mum asked me to bring her to the shop to get some food for the house in Sunderland.

As we were driving in the car, she told me she'd been diagnosed with breast cancer. I gripped the steering wheel tight; it nearly spun out of my hands.

She explained that she'd gone for a routine check-up back home in Cork and they'd discovered a small lump. Dad had been over to England a few times in the previous month for games but had kept it quiet, as mum had wanted to break the news to me herself.

The next day I was at the Sunderland training ground and headed straight to the club doctor. I started quizzing him about my mum's case… firing questions at him. I got upset and annoyed when he didn't give me the exact answers I wanted to hear.

He didn't have enough information to go on; he just tried to settle me down. It was tough news to process, a really big shock.

My mind was all over the place but when we got to Villa Park on the Wednesday night, I was focused. I was always good at that, blocking out my off- field 'life' when it came to match day and just concentrating on my job on the pitch as a midfielder.

I WAS IN control of my mind in those situations, but now injury has struck again. I feel powerless.

Dad wanted to stay on with me for another week, but mum had surgery the next day. I asked him to go home to be with her and make sure she was okay. That was the priority. He flew back to Ireland after the match. (The operation went well; mum has been fine since and goes for her regular check-ups.)

But, in Sunderland, I was in the hands of the medical team again. I needed a scan on my knee, and had to get the verdict from the surgeon and to find out what the physio's rehab plan was this time.

The aftermath of my first knee injury is a blur. It was a new situation for me and I just followed the instructions to recover. Second time around is different. I'm more informed but I don't know everything… questions started creeping into my mind.

How long am I going to be out for? Six months?

Nine? Twelve?

Can I get my knee right to play Premier League football again? Am I able, mentally, to go through all of this again?

I AM DAVID Meyler. I'm 21 years of age, and I have torn my cruciate ligament for the second time in eight months.

There are so many questions, but only one matters… I keep asking myself. *Can I come back from this?*

John Meyler: *I left Birmingham that night just as the second-half started. I was shattered as I headed up the road in the car and turned on BBC Radio 5 Live to listen in. The match commentator mentioned David for about 30 seconds. 'Having done his cruciate once and to do it again, we just wish him all the best of luck now… he'll be back.' That gave me the boost I needed. Those words stuck in my head for a long time after.*
'He will be back.'

'Where were you when John O'Shea put the ball in the German net?'

I got asked that a lot after Ireland's captain scored the 94th minute equaliser against the world champions in Gelsenkirchen on Tuesday October 14, 2014.

Where was I?

I was on the far side of the pitch, absolutely wrecked. I'd spent 90 minutes tearing around after those German fellas; put in at right-back by Martin O'Neill to fill a gap as Seamus Coleman was out injured.

We had hung in there, were only behind 1-0 and then John took his chance in injury-time. Everyone said to me after that they couldn't see me in the celebrations on the TV after John had run away towards the Irish fans; different fellas hanging off him. I just didn't have the energy to sprint across, my tank was empty.

I jogged over and got there eventually. Jeff Hendrick turned and dragged me in for the group hug.

The final whistle sounded soon after. The German players were shell-shocked, we were just walking on air.

We go back over to salute the away section; the Ireland fans stuck over by a corner flag at the Veltins-Arena. I'll never forget walking off the pitch that night. A full house… a last-minute equaliser to get us a draw… and I look up at the crowd.

I see mum and dad. There are tears in dad's eyes; he's jumping up and down, squeezing the life out of mum. After all the injuries and uncertainty and missed opportunities, it's special that they're there and able to share in that moment. Their son from Cork playing against a team that won the World Cup final three months previously in Brazil, and Ireland getting a result in the most dramatic way possible. Our emotions went through the roof.

They had a drive of over two hours after that game, heading north-west, back over the border from Germany into the Netherlands and onto Schiphol airport in Amsterdam to catch their flight home.

Over the years, dad has spent a lot of nights on the road around Ireland and England after my matches. He's covered countless miles on motorways; plenty of times when it was easy to be worried about what direction my career was going.

This time there was no worry. Just happiness and satisfaction. That night he says the car drove itself.

HULL 'Til I Die?

IT WAS A night out in London in September 2012, when the prospect of move to Hull first came up. I can clearly remember it.

I made my debut for Ireland that night, a Sunderland club player playing against Oman in Craven Cottage. Went out in London afterwards, on a high after making my international debut.

I bumped into Aaron McClean that night, he played for Hull at the time. He'd heard I'd been linked with a move there and sold me on the idea, how the club would be good for me… that I'd fit right in.

Around that time as well a group of us at Sunderland went for a game of golf one Sunday morning and ended up back in Lee Cattermole's house. Alex Bruce was there, he was playing for Hull then and I got chatting to him… he was good friends with Cattermole. Same story as McClean, Alex was saying I needed to come to Hull, how I'd enjoy it.

The 2011-12 season had been a write-off in my development.

I continued to stall in the autumn of 2012. Martin O'Neill was desperate for me to stay at the club. I put in about 10 requests for a loan move, as I wanted games with the view to coming back stronger. He turned them all down.

'No, I need you around the place!'

That was a brilliant thing to hear but it didn't change my situation. I eventually wore him down and he agreed I could go out for two months, in November 2012.

Different clubs made enquiries but Steve Bruce had taken over at Hull, and they wanted me. I had another couple of loan offers at that time… Nottingham Forest wanted me, there was talk of Leeds. But Hull were the most prominent and, ultimately, I signed for them primarily because of Steve Bruce. He was a manager I knew, and I was a player he knew.

We had respect for each other.

He called me up.

'Right… come on down here and play for us.

'This team is going to get promoted, and I could do with you midfield.'

That was enough for me. I was desperate to play football.

I DIDN'T KNOW a lot about Hull back then. It was not an area of England I was overly familiar with.

My uncle Mark is from York… he and my aunt lived there and then moved home to Cork. Growing up they would talk of where they were living, and surrounding areas like Hull would've been mentioned.

The first time the football club came across my radar was when they got promoted to the Premier League after winning the 2008 play-off final against Bristol City. I've seen the Dean Windass goal a million times from that day in Wembley… that brilliant volley after a chip across by Frazier Campbell, a player I would spend a good portion of my career with, largely as we recovered from injuries together.

I played against Hull for Sunderland in April 2010, the week before I tore my cruciate for the first time. Darren Bent scored the winner and it was the result that effectively consigned them to relegation.

So I was entering new territory in moving to Hull and needed to adjust.

2011 HAD BEEN a year of change.

That summer we went on holiday in Marbella, seven lads in a big apartment. Before heading to the beach one morning, Jordan asked me to wait on.

'I think Liverpool want to sign me.'

'WHAT?!'

It was a mad, surreal morning. He ended up cutting short the holiday and heading home early.

I was delighted for him and sad to see him go as well. He was a fella I clicked with from the start at Sunderland. He helped me settle in and I became friends with all his buddies. His father looked after me.

When I bought my house in Cottingham outside Hull, Brian Henderson viewed it first for me. We'd just got promoted and I was away that summer when these houses came on the market. Brian's not an auctioneer but was just someone I could trust. Not a problem for Brian, he drove down and sorted everything.

Brian was there the day Jordan signed, and Kenny Dalglish asked how I was recovering from my injury. He mentioned they were interested in buying the two of us together. A good few years later, I briefly talked to Kenny about it. It's a waste of energy to think about that. No one knows if it was realistic.

I feel really happy for Jordan at how he's taken his opportunity. A decade at Anfield… first-choice midfielder…captain…Champions League winner…Premier League champions. He'll go down as a legend at the club and I got to witness the start of it; the excitement as he waited in Spain that morning to get a call from his agent to confirm that one of the biggest clubs in the world wanted him.

THE OTHER BIG departure came in November.

Steve Bruce was sacked. I was gutted. The man had done so much for me. Steve was very clever when I was injured. In April 2011, he put me on the bench for an away game at Birmingham City. We both knew deep down I was nowhere near ready to play, but it was his way of recognising the hard work that was being put in.

A show of support I appreciated.

As I edged back to fitness in the 2011-12 season, I got a few runs as a sub under Steve. Then after we lost 2-1 at home to bottom of the table Wigan, he was out the door. That was Wednesday… and by Saturday Martin O'Neill had taken over.

Dad rang me straightaway.

We'd both watched his work with Celtic and he thought this was a brilliant fit; a manager who'd make me a better midfielder.

The problem was the gap between our respective needs. Martin couldn't accommodate a midfielder easing back to fitness. The pressure was on instantly to get results. People later reckoned I was in trouble when Martin was appointed

Ireland manager as he hadn't played me at Sunderland. There was more to it, to do with my fitness, and not a simple fact that Martin didn't rate me.

I understood, but was getting frustrated at playing reserve football as 2011 ended. If you've tasted the Premier League, it is a serious comedown.

A Tuesday playing somewhere like the rugby pitch at Widnes in awful weather?

More grim than glamour.

We played Man United at that time… I scored in a 6-3 win at the Eppleton Colliery Welfare Ground outside Sunderland. All our young lads were raving before about their midfielder Paul Pogba. If I was a bit dubious then about the next big thing tag, I was in no doubt after the game.

That 18-year-old was destined to be a top midfielder.

FAMILIAR FACES HELPED me out when I landed in Hull.

I knew Paul McShane from Sunderland. I couldn't speak highly enough of him. Me and Paul argued all the time, but he was a character and someone who had your back when you were in the trenches together.

Obviously at Hull, Robbie Brady signed the same day as me. He knew a lot of the Hull lads already; there was a group of them who had been together at Manchester United as kids…James Chester, Joe Dudgeon and Cameron Stewart.

There's always that thing where the Irish lads look after you. They were all good to me, and helped bring me into the squad to integrate, settle me down and make sure I was okay.

Bruce had pointed out that Hull was different to Sunderland. Take the training ground for example. The Hull City facility was not big, just a compact venue with a couple of pitches. The Sunderland set-up at that time was incredible with the array of pitches, top-class gym facilities and a swimming pool. Years later, I remember talking to Brucey about it and he said he didn't like the place. It was too big and sprawling, people could go hiding he felt. The manager's office was at one end of the building, and you could spend the day well away from it.

I remember my agent telling me when I joined Hull that I should head to the training pitch the first day. I stayed outside Hull the night before, the Humber View Hotel in North Ferriby. Next morning, I whacked the postcode in for directions from the hotel and drove towards it in Cottingham.

I'm driving away, and then I see this little gate blocking a narrow laneway up to where I was being directed to. It was an old bowls club with two pitches. Given from where I'd been with Sunderland and their state-of-the-art complex, this took a bit of getting used to. It reminded me more of Cork City's facility back home in Bishopstown in Ireland.

Basic, no frills attached.

In Sunderland, I had my own locker with name and photo plastered across it. I walked into the changing room in Hull the first day... blue walls, planks of wood for you sit on that ran right around the room. A peg on the wall with a top and bottom hook to be shared between two players for hanging their clothes.

It was a culture shock that first day.

I walked out of the dressing-room and realised I could clearly hear the manager having a chat in the canteen. There was no avoiding anyone in this place. No hiding spots. You were forced to see every player, every coach and every staff member... *every day.*

Over time the place changed slightly.

When we got promotion first, Brucey ordered the changing rooms to get a makeover... everyone got their own locker. There was a poster of the player above it to signify it was yours. That worked as players were sticking around a good bit, but after a while there was such chopping and changing, they went to a number system on the lockers.

I've been back there since and it's still similar. There's been a portakabin extension to the gym but no major differences.

The whole set-up worked, though. It made me realise a football club doesn't need a huge, fancy complex. We had two great pitches, and the groundsmen put in a lot of work to make sure they were top quality. Most fellas bought into it straightaway. If someone joined from a big club, they got a surprise initially as they weren't expecting it. They quickly got on board, however... the narrow corridors, the tables for eating where everyone was sharing space. It was intimate and we grew close.

When we were flying high going for promotion or on a good run in the cup, the buzz around the place was just brilliant every day when we went to training.

There was something romantic about it... a real down to earth place, I guess.

THERE WERE NO real reservations on my part about joining Hull.

Dad's opinion was the main one that I sought out. He was a bit uncertain about this voluntary drop down a division, but he got on board quickly enough, thinking that Bruce was there… 'He said you're going to play, so away you go'.

No doubts.

Bruce was manager and he vowed we'd get promoted. I trusted him and wanted to be a part of it. Hull were fourth in the table at the time I joined on loan and had a good Irish group at the club.

It was the right time to make the move.

When I moved to Hull in the autumn of 2012 from Sunderland (right), I could never have imagined that within two years I would be out on the hallowed turf of Wembley and playing against Arsenal in the FA Cup final.

2

Dad and Me

MAYBE MY SPORTING obsession was inevitable.

My mum Stella is a wonderful swimmer, and a good golfer. She's taken up bridge in recent years; the competitiveness shows there as well.

I've just one sibling, my sister Sarah. Three years between us… she was born in 1986 and I arrived in '89. Sarah was a serious swimmer too, growing up. Dad still says he should have sent her off to England to a specialised swimming school because he felt she hit a ceiling in Ireland. After finishing secondary school, she went to Limerick to study to become a teacher. She's principal now in St Iberius National School in Wexford town.

Then, there is dad.

JOHN MEYLER IS a name familiar to many in Irish sport.

In Ireland, the national sports are gaelic football and hurling. Dad has spent his life wrapped up in them, particularly in hurling. As a player he was a hurler for the Wexford and Cork county senior teams. He also captained his club St Finbarr's to an All-Ireland senior football title in 1987.

Then, when he retired, he turned his hand to management. My whole life I've known him to be managing and coaching hurling teams. Big, significant sides in Ireland like the Cork and Wexford hurlers, and then club teams like Kilmoyley in Kerry, where he has enjoyed great success. He has played an enormous role in shaping my life, right from when I started out as a footballer.

Dad grew up in Wexford in the south-east of Ireland. My grandparents were busy hard-working people… ran a farm, a pub, a shop and a filling station. In amidst all that, dad was allowed to pursue his sporting passions. My grandfather played cricket in the local leagues in Wexford between the villages and he kept greyhounds as well, running them in tracks in the county.

He was interested when my dad started playing hurling, making sure he had whatever gear or equipment was needed. Then dad used to say his mother would always make sure he was prepared for whatever training session he had on in the evening. He was told mid-afternoon on the farm to stop working, to go in and wash himself, have some food and get ready for training.

Dad said that to earn his father's respect, you had to play well.

Same story with me and him. Dad learned not to shower me with praise if I'd been poor… always be totally straight. That honesty was important.

When I was younger, he bought me a pool table, an old style one that you'd see in pubs which needed the 20 pence coin slotted in. We'd play, and he'd never let me win… the usual tears and tantrums as a child when I was beaten.

Age didn't matter. There were no handouts.

It did make me practice pool non-stop. Later when I was in England, trying to make my way as a professional footballer, I was still using the lessons from those pool games. You earn everything you get. If you lose, then you need to get better.

Sport dominated my youth. I swam a bit but just wasn't a big fan of getting up at 6am to jump into a pool. There were lots of summer days spent at Douglas Golf Club. And then I'd the big three!

Hurling with Blackrock.

Gaelic football with St Michael's.

Football with College Corinthians.

I loved the variety, and the beauty was that I learned so much from each sport. Hurling taught me how to take a belt. Playing football in England, I would get clattered but could take the hit where other fellas were rolling around the field.

Gaelic football came most naturally to me.

Football, or soccer as we say in Ireland, helped with my ability to think during a game, watching formations and how teams were set-up. Of the three, I feel hurling was the game I was best at.

I fully believe I'd have played for the Cork senior hurling team if I'd stuck at it. That may sound arrogant, but it is a genuine belief. In Blackrock, in Cork, there was no shortage of hurling heroes growing up. The backbone of the county winning teams... the Brownes, the Cashmans, Wayne Sherlock, Brian O'Keeffe... Fergal Ryan. We loved having underage games when the seniors were training and we were wondering would they be watching.

Then we'd all get the bus down to Páirc Uí Chaoimh to see the Rockies seniors play. But my No.1 hurling hero growing up was from East Cork.

We're all glory-hunters when we're kids, so we gravitate towards one forward. Joe Deane was this five feet and six inches scoring machine. He floated around popping over points and I loved watching him. His free-taking style was distinctive, hunched low over the ball with the hurley positioned between his legs before he would lift and strike.

Joe had a yellow Cooper helmet. So, I badly wanted one as well.

My helmet was a blue Mycro.

I used to pester dad. He eventually sorted me a green Gola helmet. I came downstairs one morning... it was there on the island in the kitchen. That was more valuable for trading.

I managed to swap it for a yellow Cooper.

When I got to play in Semple Stadium in 2002, I'd the yellow Cooper and red jersey on a big hurling day, just like Joe Deane.

I WAS A slave to sporting fashion in other ways too. Adidas Predators were the kings of boots. I still have about 12 pairs in the garage. One day I want to get into management and I think I'll wear them. A good luck charm.

When we were younger, the new releases would drop in Cummins Sports in Douglas. The Manias came out around the 2002 World Cup... they cost €192. Everyone wanted them. I watched all the Cork players who had them... Seán Óg and John Gardiner for the hurlers... Colin Corkery with the white ones for the footballers.

We'd a match with St Michael's that summer. Eric Hegarty's mum drove up beforehand and handed him a pair of boots. She'd queued up... now he was wearing the Manias. I was insanely jealous, so I went home after and started to make the case to dad that these boots will make me play better. He set up one of his 'challenge and reward' systems over a few games… then got me the boots.

I looked the part. They're my favourite boot of all time. When Hull played Wolves in 2017, I scored a penalty late in the game in injury-time and had those boots on. I'm retired now but if adidas put them back for resale, I'd probably buy three or four pairs anyway. I was fortunate to have the support where dad would shell out nearly €200 on a pair of boots for a 13-year-old.

Thankfully, I paid him back over the years.

THE SUMMER OF 2002, I captained Cork in the Kennedy Cup, a national under-13 competition in Limerick in Ireland. That tournament is a milestone if you're developing as a young Irish footballer.

Want to get noticed? That's the national stage to impress, with scouts dotted all over the pitches in Limerick. Talk of Ireland call-ups began.

We were young lads, who had made the grade at under-13 with Cork, but then came the next challenge. Trials with Ireland teams. There were four of us from Corinthian Boys – myself, David Bevan, Richard O'Donovan and Jamie Drennan – who would make the trip up to Dublin every few months. Teenagers trying to shine in auditions… keep our sporting dreams alive. I was the only one who wasn't capped underage. The lads all played under-15 for Ireland.

Never getting that opportunity was frustrating. There was a Dublin bubble you had to break through. A Dublin management team and a Dublin-based squad. That was just the way it was run. The best schoolboy players from around the country moved there; you bettered your case to get into the Ireland squad if you went playing in Dublin.

It has progressed now into a better situation. I'm involved with the Ireland under-17 coaching team and if young players are on the rise around the country, we'll find out about them. The best players are picked regardless of where they're from. At that age, rejection is tough to take.

The lads came back home to Cork with their Ireland gear. I was that guy who went up with them and returned with nothing.

Dad used to contact the Ireland management in search of answers, but nothing came of it. I was lucky that my father didn't try and live a career through me. He'd regularly ask did I want to pursue professional football and then he worked to provide every opportunity when I'd say I did.

He'd open the door and say, 'There… go walk through it!' Some fathers are pulling the young fella through the door.

We laugh about that time now.

In my life, I played for and captained the Ireland senior team.

Getting the cold shoulder at underage was all part of the journey to reach my destination.

COLLEGE CORINTHIANS WAS where I started playing football; my local club just up the road in Castletreasure. The team I played for won everything in Cork up through the underage ranks. The National Cup was always a step too far for us; we could never manage to beat some of the top Dublin sides.

We spent thrilling years together, however… full of wonder.

Richard O'Donovan, Theo Cullinane, David O'Sullivan, Steven Good, Eoghan McCarthy, Jamie Drennan… the backbone of our team. A lot of lads had trials with English clubs. Our goalkeeper David Bevan signed for Aston Villa, and had a couple of loan moves after that. Ian Turner carved out a career with Cork City and then went to Cobh Ramblers.

Barry O'Driscoll was a year younger but played with us numerous times. One of those lads gifted at sport, he was like a gazelle on the pitch with his pace. He went down another sporting path, made it with the Cork senior footballers and is still going strong at a high level with Nemo Rangers.

There was no big mystery to where I ended up playing gaelic games, I just followed my friends. We lived in Rochestown, but used to go to school in Beaumont. All the lads in my class were playing with Blackrock in hurling and St Michael's in football. It was a no-brainer.

I wanted to be playing with all my friends. Every day we'd go to my grandparents' house… Blackrock's club pitches on Church Road were just across the road. A simple decision.

In Beaumont, we were really successful at GAA but by sixth class I had changed schools to St Anthony's in Ballinlough. A bit hot-headed in the classroom, not paying enough attention, it was felt the switch would be good for me. Dad got me in, having talked to the principal Flor O'Sullivan.

I played GAA there and scored 2-2 when we reached the Sciath na Scol hurling final in 2002. I also got sent-off after cleaning a player out with a hurley as I tried to strike the ball. It wasn't intentional, but a wild enough pull meant I was gone.

It didn't tarnish my hurling record too badly as I got picked for the 'Primary Game' team to play Waterford that year, before the senior match in Semple Stadium. Noel Connors, the future Waterford defender, marked me that day, but I got a couple of goals off him.

I WAS SURROUNDED by plenty of talented players growing up. Eric Hegarty was gifted at all three sports, played Cork minor football and still plays for Michael's. Declan Kelleher and Brian Ahern were excellent too.

Then there was Simon Zebo… a famous sporting product who would go on to star as a winger at the highest stage of professional rugby.

Simon is a year younger than me but we were pals growing up on the same Blackrock and St Michael's teams. He'd plenty of natural GAA talent but went off and made a name for himself in rugby with Munster and Ireland. Then off out to France for a few years to live his best life before a homecoming to Munster.

What you see with him in public is what you get in private. A lovely fella. Always bubbly and smiling. A great character. He always had that X-Factor on the pitch… in every sport. The famous flick against Wales in the Six Nations in 2013 reminded me how he just played like that naturally all his life. His ability to think on his feet in situations on a pitch was always incredible… he'd stay calm-headed when everyone was panicking.

We'd be good friends. We wouldn't speak every day, but we catch up every now and then.

ON THE FOOTBALL field, I was always a centre midfielder. My best attribute was winning the ball back… 'the rat' as it would be classed in midfield terms, the type who get the ball and give it off to the more creative players.

In hurling, I always wanted to play centre-forward. I wasn't the best striker off my right but I probably was clean off the left. I was hot-headed as a young fella. Had an argument with my dad once during a county semi-final with Blackrock… point down and we'd a late free.

I said go for goal… he said take your point. I took his advice.

We won the replay.

As I got older some coaches understood I wanted to combine my sports. We were very successful with St Michael's. I'll never forget the influence of Gerry Lenihan. If I missed training, there was no problem with Gerry. He knew he could count on me. If my parents were away, he would call over to bring me to and from training.

I feel that sense of appreciation with all my coaches. John Turner and Danny Drennan with our Corinthians team, different people in Blackrock. Those younger days back in Cork, when I was switching between sports every week, gave me some of my happiest memories.

EVERYONE SEEMED TO support Man United when we were younger, so I joined Gavin Dempsey in school in supporting Liverpool.

We wanted to be different.

Dad wouldn't support clubs, but he loves teams from different eras… Leeds in the 70s, Liverpool in the 80s. He bought me the old v-neck Liverpool jersey with Carlsberg emblazoned across the front.

The player I worshipped didn't play for Liverpool, yet that was never going to affect my devotion. In Cork at that time, there was a clear choice.

Roy Keane was a Cork native, Manchester United captain and Ireland's best player. *How could I not be inspired by that?* He had everything as a midfielder. An exceptional passer and goal-scorer. His determination, the way he tackled… and led his team.

I was never glued to watching games on TV, and preferred to watch the *Match of the Day* round-ups. But I wish I'd studied the game more; analysed players like Roy properly. Later, I found him really helpful when I got to work with him. Playing in similar positions influenced my fanaticism. I captained Cork in the Kennedy Cup, just like Roy did in 1986. Every year when the team is picked, someone gets touted as the next Roy Keane.

But you'll go another hundred years and there won't be another player from Cork to match up to Roy. He's out on his own.

BY THE AGE of 15, I faced questions. *What was my football ambition and how could it be fulfilled?*

My good fortune was to have a father who looked at the bigger picture. Corinthians was a well-run club but dominating at your own age group creates a comfort zone. Dad felt it was time for a move. So, when I was under-15, I moved to Cobh Ramblers. A bigger challenge.

The weekend schedule was intense. On a Saturday the under-15s would play at 11am... then I'd kick off with the under-17s at 2pm. Sunday morning was the under-16s, and the under-18 team that afternoon. Four games, but I was energetic and eager to play ball.

Cobh was a positive place to play. Graham Cummins was two years older but we played together underage. A traditional centre-forward with an eye for goal, he played later in England and Scotland, and shone for Cork City.

Cobh's first-team were in the League of Ireland. Sometimes you'd train with them; they were good lads. I was the young, fresh-faced kid but they didn't let me away with anything. They all wanted me to raise my standards.

Dad used to set me a challenge.

The match reports would be brief in the local paper, the *Evening Echo*. To get mentioned, you needed to score a goal. Hitting the net was the challenge and €50 for every goal the proposed reward.

That prize drove me on. One weekend, I scored nine goals across four games; pushing to take free-kicks and penalties. He paid up every time but, eventually, it had to stop. The initial aim was for more recognition, now I was emptying his wallet.

Dad was asking me if I wanted to reach the top, and then mapping out what was required.

It goes back to the lesson of the pool table battles. Or when he'd send me down to the Rochestown College handball alley, where many Cork hurlers have honed their skills over the years. I would be handed a new sliotar to bang it against a wall for a few hours... before he'd see how battered it was and determine how much work I'd done. There were free-taking sessions in Church Road after he'd collect me from my nan's… 80 to 100 frees all from different angles. If I hit a target number, we'd stop at McDonalds on the way home.

Dad would later describe the strategy as almost a sort of bribery, something designed to keep me going at sport, retain my focus. Whether it was a new hurley, a pair of boots, a football I wanted, a few quid for the wallet… there was a prize introduced for achievement as I developed as a youth. All these things used as sporting motivations.

Then it was up to me to respond and earn it.

There was another key person in all of this. Mum did the driving up and down to Cobh a few times a week. She'd rearrange things in her life to do that. Make sure I was eating right and all my gear was washed. Always there, always involved.

But I never felt a weight of parental pressure.

I wanted to do it and they helped steer me in the right direction.

SOMETIMES, I THINK I'd love another shot at secondary school.

Just to enjoy the moments and put some work in. I went to Christian Brothers College in Cork and got in plenty of trouble. Stupid stuff, messing in class and getting thrown out. Tony McCarthy was the vice-principal… he'd be ringing dad every second week.

The principal Dr Larry Jordan knew I was sports mad. In Christians, the main focus was rugby; he used to be on to me to play. They thought they could have a full-back or winger on their hands. But I'd no interest.

You couldn't escape the rugby tradition in the school all the same. Duncan Williams, Stephen Archer and John Ryan were all in the years ahead of me… they all later played for Munster.

The games were massive occasions and I went to them all. All my classmates were playing. I did envy them their sporting routine… team meetings, having lunch together, training after school.

I was outside that bubble. I was desperate as a teenager to be part of an elite sporting culture. And soon enough I got my chance.

DAMIEN RICHARDSON WAS the Cork City first-team manager. He was an experienced figure in Irish football. A Dubliner, he'd played and managed Gillingham in England while also taking various jobs managing major teams in Ireland.

In July 2007, he came up to me after a game where I had played for the Cork City under-21 team. We chatted about the match. I had played well… he praised my performance. Then came one of the most pivotal questions I was asked in my life.

'What are you doing next Monday night?'

My mind started racing.

'We're playing Sunderland… I want you to be involved. You'll get some minutes.'

The chance to play against a Premier League team. Roy Keane was their manager. Turner's Cross was sold out. There was just one slight issue. A fixture clash… I had a gaelic football minor championship game with St Michael's.

Monday night football.

But where was I going to play?

THAT JULY WAS a crazy month.

On Sunday July 1, I was in Killarney with the Cork minor footballers as we beat Kerry in the Munster final. On Sunday July 8, I played for the Cork City under-21s that beat the Kerry League in a cup game in Tralee.

On Sunday July 15, I lined out centre-forward and scored a goal as the Blackrock intermediate hurlers beat St Finbarr's in a relegation play-off in Páirc Uí Rinn. Then, to cap off the month, I'd to wrestle with this decision of where to go on Monday July 31. It summed up the madness of the time.

No 18-year-old would get away with that schedule now. I was still living the dream, getting to play three sports I loved.

I just about managed to keep them going but issues did arise.

It was my downfall with the Cork minor footballers. I got called into a trial match down in Kinsale once and tore the whole place up, scoring a few goals.

'We're very pleased with how you've done,' said the manager Mick Evans after. 'We want to bring you into the squad. How are you fixed for Saturday?'

'Ah, I think I've a soccer match.'

That was the problem. When we won the Munster final, I was the Cork water boy in Fitzgerald Stadium. I hadn't been available enough to be picked, but packing in soccer wasn't an option.

That Cork team had serious talent. The half-forward line was Barry O'Driscoll, Ciaran Sheehan and Aidan Walsh, all future senior footballers.

Sliding doors moments.

I didn't play for the Cork minor team that day and didn't play for the St Michael's minors at the end of July either. Damien Richardson pushed me into making a choice. I knew whichever I picked, the other would be affected.

Dad asked, 'Well, what do you want to do?'

I was nearly hoping he'd make the decision for me. I hung my hat on going the soccer route.

Being part of the Cork City first-team squad was one attraction but the glamour of the opposition was another. And Roy Keane was in charge, his big homecoming to Cork. *Was there a chance I could get to meet him?*

I've often wondered was there a plan hatched in the background at Cork City. *Were the youth coaches worried about losing a player to GAA? Did they feel I needed some big offer to commit?*

Not everyone was happy with my decision. A few lads with St Michael's felt I'd let them down and fell out with me for a couple of years. They won that night, but lost the county semi-final later in November. I missed that due to soccer as well.

We made up. We got over it. That's part of sport.

And at least I went on to do something.

I got brought on with 10 minutes to go that night against Sunderland. A brief window to impress; I'm not sure if I even touched the ball. But still, I was sharing a pitch with Premier League stars. And I got a photo with Roy after.

I still have the photo and I showed it to Roy years later when we were together with Ireland. 'Can't believe I'm actually smiling!' That was his verdict.

He would go on to be a huge influence in my career. He signed me for Sunderland. He was one of the first people to get in touch when I suffered the cruciate injuries. Same situation when I retired.

It's stuff that people don't know about him. They see this fella ranting on a sideline or as a tough-talking pundit in a TV studio… and think… *Roy Keane.*

There's a decency at his core.

I THINK PEOPLE in the football community in Cork always thought I was leaning towards GAA. Given my dad's background, it was felt I would go that way. It is a wonderful achievement to play for Cork, but football can be your profession.

That's what appealed to me, not having to combine sport with a job. That's why I was so fascinated with football.

The first approach from Cork City came in the summer of 2006. Paul Bowdren spotted me when they played Cobh. He rang dad about having a chat with us. So, we met him in O'Briens' sandwich shop in Douglas Court Shopping Centre. He mapped out the path for us… paid for our sandwiches after, a good first impression.

I was eligible to play under-17 but he viewed me as a signing for the under-18s. That's what dad wanted to hear; they talked about me getting some game-time for the under-21s as well. This was a sign of taking a step up. Bowdy was brilliant for me when I was at Cork City. He'd facilitate me if I couldn't train at times. A really good guy who I kept in touch with.

When I was younger, dad would sometimes bring me to Cork City games at Turner's Cross. The team of Declan Daly, John Caulfield and Patsy Freyne! As I got older, I went to fewer games but would still look out for their results. By the time I signed I was no fanatic… I wasn't at the back of The Shed every week, singing… *Cork City 'Til die.*

But it was still a big deal to sign for them.

When I started to train with the first-team, it was a dressing-room with big midfield names… Colin Healy and Gareth Farrelly… Joe Gamble.

In an early training session, Colin hit me a belt of a shoulder and knocked me into next week. I was coming in as this cocky 17-year-old, used to games working out easily. He forced me to understand what was required. There were times I flew into tackles with him and I think he respected that. Colin was hard on me but in the right way, so I would learn.

If training was at 9am, Colin was at the ground an hour earlier. Making sure his boots were clean, his gear was ready… he had his stretching done and organised in the gym. After training he'd do extra work on passing and finishing. Then back into the gym.

He set the bar. Colin had two bad leg breaks. You don't come back from them and play at the level he did without having something about you. I took great inspiration from him.

Joe had been at Reading; he had soaked up a lot from his time there, and was the first player to introduce me to the concept of going into the gym for activation work before training… passed on lessons about nutrition, hydration and warming up. He was built like a tank. His reading of the game was excellent. You see midfielders charging around the pitch. Joe chose when to charge and when not to charge.

When I was younger, I was more interested in the fella doing the step-overs or scoring goals. Now, I was trying to learn more about positional play. Roy Keane would later be great for advice on that.

If the ball is in front of you, you've done your job.

Everyone at times is so quick to press, but the higher level you go up, the better the players are and they'll pop the ball around you.

When you're running back to your own goal and the ball is gone behind you, then you know you're in trouble.

Colin and Joe guided me along. The Cork City squad went to Spain for a warm-weather training camp in February 2008. I was a few months out from my 19th birthday. At the end of the week, we'd a night out in Marbella.

Everyone was having a few drinks; then Colin and Joe pulled me aside, sat me down and grilled me for 20 minutes about what I was doing.

'You've got potential, but you need to straighten your head out.'

Time to cut out the outside noise. If we played on a Friday night and my buddies were going out after, I should be thinking about playing the under-21 game on the Saturday.

They displayed unbelievable faith in me; tried to steer a young player on the right path, correct my mistakes. I'll be forever grateful to them.

Maybe they saw something of themselves at that age in me; felt it was time to share the wisdom. There is a spiral effect in football. I'm involved now with Ireland under-17s, because Colin O'Brien, who was at Cork City back then, was very good to me when I retired in reaching out and opening that door. A very open-minded person, who always had an interest in coaching.

And now, I find myself talking to young fellas, passing on some advice just like Colin and Joe did for me all those years ago.

GEORGE O'CALLAGHAN WAS the other Cork City player that stood out with his talent.

Georgie was a maverick.

The game came naturally to him. He'd do all sorts of tricks in training. We used to do a version of the crossbar challenge. At the old Bishopstown ground where Cork City train, there was a metal frame in the shape of goalposts that you'd walk under coming out from the dressing-rooms.

George would offer me €100 if I could hit it… and give me three balls from the centre circle. Then he'd join in after my shots and if he got it, I'd have to clean his boots. I'd miss my three and then he'd bang it first go.

I was left cleaning his boots.

He was a special talent in the League of Ireland.

Could George have done more?

I think so. He was a larger-than-life character and incredibly gifted.

In the company of the legendary GAA star Jimmy Barry Murphy (top left) after Cork regained the Liam MacCarthy Cup in 1999; and (top right) working as a 'water boy' during the Munster minor football final in Killarney in 2007. Me and dad celebrate (below) after he led Cork to the Munster Hurling Championship title in 2018.

A Dream Begins

IRELAND RECOGNITION EVENTUALLY arrived in March 2008.

On a Tuesday night I played in Waterford against France in an under-19 international. It had been a long wait. First-team status with Cork City had validated me in a way and helped ensure the call was made. You have to show you're at a certain level to get in the team. That you deserve your spot.

I came on as a second-half substitute. Moussa Sissoko and Morgan Schneiderlin were future Premier League names in that French midfield, but it was Gabriel Obertan who ripped us apart. He scored a couple of lovely goals that night and the following year Man United signed him.

Once I made the under-19 squad, I felt I had to leave a lasting mark. Seán McCaffrey was the manager and I wanted him to remember me that week. Dad used to say whatever time team events are, be there way before everyone else.

We ate with the French team, in one big massive conference room in a Waterford hotel. Breakfast was at 9am… I was sitting at the table by 8am. Seán was the second person down. I'd always be there waiting and we'd chat away.

For team meetings, I made sure to be there 45 minutes early. I'd leave whoever I was rooming with and get in there before the video analyst was setting up. I had waited, coped with the underage rejection, but now I was prepared and ready.

We had a meeting in Cork before the second game against France a few days later. Seán put the team up. I was starting in Turner's Cross. The news left me a little dazed. He called me out in that distinctive Monaghan accent. 'David, why are you starting?'

'Eh… because you picked me.'

'No, it's because you're a good player. That's why you're starting.'

That was the validation from someone I had respect for and looked up to. It stuck with me for a long time. I really enjoyed playing for Seán. He passed away in late-2017. He had a big impact on people with small gestures, was loved and respected by players, and just one of the good fellas.

THE DESPERATION TO play for Ireland was always there. I think it's there for everyone in the country growing up with a football interest; the national team is the goal. There is a photo at home where I'm in my USA 94 kit, but World Cup 2002 is the first big international tournament that registered with me.

Roy Keane was at the peak of his powers then. Everything he did for club and country was huge news.

Saipan is a national obsession, and I think it always will be. The fascination lies in the unknown. Ireland lost in the last 16 on penalties and haven't been back to a World Cup since. *How far would we have gone if Roy was there?* At the time he was in the top five midfielders in the world… Ireland's captain and best player.

I've never talked about it with Roy. Being honest, you wouldn't know if it's a topic he's interested in revisiting.

PLAYING IRELAND UNDER-19 was great, but stepping up to under-21 football was a total different kettle of fish. I'd a new manager, was fighting with older fellas for game-time and my own background had changed as I'd joined Sunderland.

My first under-21 cap is cool to reflect on.

In February 2009, Ireland played Germany in Turner's Cross. Playing in my hometown was great with all my family at the game. Being the local lad playing is cool, but you need to perform.

I came in late to the starting team after James McCarthy got injured, and we drew 1-1. Germany had a class team; they later won the Euro under-21s that summer. Kevin-Prince Boateng was their household name, playing with Spurs at the time, and he ran the midfield. But Manuel Neuer, Jerome Boateng and Sami

Khedira quickly became the stars. The following year the three of them were in the World Cup semi-final against Spain in South Africa. In 2014, they were all involved as Germany won it in Brazil.

That was the beauty of international football. I enjoyed measuring myself against players and tracking where they went after. We beat Spain the following month, 2-1 in Waterford. Dani Parejo, with Real Madrid then, was their player tipped to go all the way. César Azpilicueta and Jordi Alba were two that jump out from that Spain team. We didn't have much success at under-21 with Don Givens, no major tournament qualification. I did strike up some great friendships in that team, however. Seamus Coleman started right-back that night against Spain.

I watched his debut for Everton later that year against Benfica, a 5-0 loss in the Europa League. He played left-back and was all over the place. A tough start. But his strength of character has always been there. I'd describe him as the stereotypical corner-back in the GAA world. Flaking into someone before the ref throws in the ball.

I know he played centre-back for Killybegs… I imagine he was horrible to mark. He was raw starting out in football, but matured and developed into such a good full-back.

IN MAY 2010 I tore my cruciate on a Sunday afternoon against Man United. On the Friday my agent had rung to say I was going to get named in the next Ireland squad for the upcoming friendlies against Paraguay and Algeria. When my knee went, it was one of those thoughts that flashed across my mind soon after. The Ireland dream was on hold.

I was the first of our group to get called up, but then had to watch the lads all my age all break into the squad. I was as excited as everyone else before Ireland played in Euro 2012.

The country got caught up in the hype. There was so much hope in Ireland but it was all wiped away by the results. They got pumped by an exceptional Spain team, with Croatia and Italy winning either side of that. I felt that team was at a turning point and opportunities would open up in the squad.

We played Swansea away with Sunderland in September. That morning in the hotel, Martin O'Neill came up to me. Good news, I made the Ireland senior squad. I was trying to take it in. Two and a half years waiting for this chance. John

O'Shea was sitting next to me; it was good to have another Irish player there.

He was congratulating me, but also reassuring. That was John, always cool, level-headed and looking out for people. Ten days later I was making my senior debut for Ireland. Playing Oman at Craven Cottage isn't the stuff of dreams but the setting and opposition didn't bother me. This was a lifetime's ambition.

We won 4-1; Robbie Brady made his debut as well and marked it with a goal.

It felt a proper debut, the full 90 minutes from the start instead of a token few at the end. I was pumped afterwards. Kept thinking… *Don't be one and done.* The single cap wonders that no one ever hears of again.

I was determined to achieve more.

I LOVED SENIOR international football from the start.

People knock smaller countries, like Oman and Gibraltar. But I always felt I was facing the best available players from that country. As proud a moment for them, as it was for us. It never became a chore hopping on a plane and heading to Dublin. It shouldn't be and if it ever does, you should get out.

We have a lot of fellas nowadays who are English with Irish heritage, but I feel the majority of them do love it. When I looked at the squads I was in, there were no real bad eggs. Ciaran Clark is a great example. He was born in England, his mother is from Leitrim and his father's family come from Donegal. He's fully into it, you couldn't doubt his passion for Ireland. Some lads don't buy into it.

Take Irish football's high-profile departures of Jack Grealish and Declan Rice. I know Declan well. He made the call to declare for England in February 2019. The previous summer we'd played together twice against Turkey and France.

I always felt in my heart he was gone.

Taking that long to decide his future was a bad sign for Ireland. I think he was buying himself enough time to play well with West Ham, establish himself and see could he get into the England squad. I don't doubt that he had affection for Ireland but his loyalties lay with England. It was his decision. I fully respected it and wished him all the best.

At the time, I came out on Twitter expressing that sentiment and got slaughtered for it. If that's what he wanted, it was the right call. I don't want fellas in the Ireland squad that aren't properly invested. He was a competitor for my position but that wasn't my motivation.

Identity is a complex topic but I think if you get any senior cap, you shouldn't be able to change your mind afterwards. People ask me about my son, and if he ends up playing football? He'd be eligible to play for Scotland through his grandfather, Ireland through me and England through my wife. *Who should he play for?*

If he's talented enough, it's his decision.

Everything was spot on when Declan was with Ireland. He trained well, applied himself correctly in games. But then England came up and his mind started to wander.

The whole mess dragged on. Once he made his decision and left, there was no point for Irish football in wasting time thinking about it.

GIOVANNI TRAPATTONI'S TIME in charge of Ireland didn't end well. The buzz before the Euros was well gone and we didn't have a good crack at reaching the World Cup in Brazil. I was in and out of squads; sitting on the bench in October 2012 when Germany ripped us apart 6-1… Özil, Reus and Kroos running riot.

Minutes were hard to come by under Trapattoni. Between my debut and when he left as Ireland manager, I got three more caps. Substitute appearances against the Faroe Islands, Greece and Spain. Combined, it was less than 30 minutes.

I didn't have much interaction with him. I think he did rate me because he put me in the squad, but he was very stuck in his ways in general and changed little. He didn't have a lot of English, so communicating to get feedback was an issue. Marco Tardelli had a better grasp of it.

With Trapattoni, I wasn't focused on him leaving but then when he did, you start to wonder who'll come in as Ireland manager.

When Martin O'Neill replaced him, I was really excited. We'd worked together at Sunderland, so there was a connection. Dad was wary; he felt Martin didn't play me then and nothing would change with Ireland.

I looked at it differently. My fitness levels were now high, my knee was good. I was a regular with Hull; in that 2013-14 season I played 30 times in the Premier League and 27 were from the start.

The chemistry was right, I was sure the international opportunities would come.

IF 2013 WAS frustrating with Ireland, 2014 turned in my favour. We'd had a long season with Hull reaching the FA Cup final. A week later we played Turkey in Dublin; a week after that was Italy in London; then Costa Rica and Portugal on a USA tour.

You hear stories of players drained from club activities and having no enthusiasm. That wasn't my attitude. I was never an Ireland regular in my career so my hunger to play always stayed high.

When I was injured, I used to stare sort of longingly at Ireland squad announcements. When fit, I wasn't turning down the chance. Every squad I was available for, bar Martin's first two, I was in. If there was a game and I was injured, I'd travel anyway, be in and around the hotel and squad. I had this real need to be a part of it.

BY AUTUMN 2014, it was time for the serious business.

No more friendlies, the Euro qualifiers were the main tests. The road to France began for us in Tbilisi, and Aiden McGeady dug it out with a magic winner against Georgia. In October, we had two games in four days against Gibraltar and Germany. Seamus was out injured… that posed an issue. Martin floated the idea with me of playing right-back just before the Gibraltar game. I was happy to do a job.

It was one of those nights you feel fortunate Robbie Keane is in your team. He had scored a hat-trick by the 18th minute; that settled any nerves I had about an unfamiliar position. It was an easy game to play and we won 7-0.

That was the trial. Playing at home against Gibraltar is one thing. Playing away against the World Cup winners was another. We flew to Germany to play on a Tuesday night in Gelsenkirchen. Martin pulled me aside on the morning of the game.

'You're okay to play right-back again tonight, yeah?'

It was as casual as that. Martin displayed great faith in me.

He could have found someone else. He knew I wasn't going to set the world alight but that I would pour my heart and soul into it. At Sunderland I lined out a couple of times at centre-half for Martin. I think he knew I'd slot into a gap and give him everything. Adrenaline helps get you through it.

As do great teammates.

I was so lucky. Jon Walters played right wing and John O'Shea was right side centre-half. People say I played solidly but it was all down to them. Sheasy shouting all night.

'LEFT!'

'RIGHT!'

'PUSH UP!'

'DROP BACK!'

He talked me through the game. Walters covered anytime I was in bother, that engine of his motoring all night long.

Germany had special players. Karim Bellarabi was left wing, Toni Kroos controlled everything in the middle. Julian Draxler started and Lukas Podolski came on. Thomas Müller and Mario Götze were always dangerous.

At one stage they all piled over to my wing, popping one-twos around me. It was almost hypnotising to see up close.

I didn't feel over-awed though. You have to cherish the moment and live in it. Rise to the challenge, make sure the game will not pass you by. At one stage, Podolski slipped in and shaped to shoot. I'd played against him... he'd scored twice for Arsenal against Hull the previous April.

I dived at the ball and he volleyed the side of my head. Don't be the one that messes up here... that was my aim. We couldn't hold out and Kroos put them ahead 1-0 with 20 minutes left.

Then, into the 93rd minute and McGeady takes the ball near the corner flag and rolls it back to Wes Hoolahan. I was a few yards away as a passing option but there's no way I was getting the ball. These are the situations Wes takes control of, whipping in crosses.

He pumped it too long and it was only later the realisation hit of how well Jeff Hendrick did; following the flight of the ball, swivelling and sending it back across the box. Then it's all about John O'Shea on his 100th cap having the drive to get ahead of Mats Hummels, put out his right leg and score one of Irish football's most famous goals.

It's the greatest equaliser I've ever been part of on the pitch. The mad joy of the team celebrating, the happiness when we all got to the dressing-room, and the emotion at seeing my parents after.

I'm in the middle of it all. No Ireland underage career to speak of, waiting until 2008 for an international debut... until 2012 for a first senior cap.

Then, this magical night in Gelsenkirchen.

It showed the value of sticking at it. I'm a firm believer that your mind is an amazing thing if you set it towards a goal. You just need to figure out your levels of desire and determination. I'd been knocking on the door for Ireland for so long and, that night, it felt I had forced my way through.

A young me with my dreams and beardless (top left) on Ireland under-21 duty in 2010 in a European qualifier against Armenia, and (top right) in action in the same game.

My international career ended in Wroclaw in September 2018 after a friendly against Poland.

4

School's Out

AT THE START of fifth year, at the time I joined Cork City, I switched schools. Left Christians and moved to Bruce College, swapping Sidney Hill for St Patrick's Hill on the northside. The hope was that it would give me better focus.

Micheál Landers was the principal at Bruce. He was brilliant for facilitating my soccer commitments, particularly at the start of Leaving Cert year. School started at 8.40am. An hour later I'd drive out to Bishopstown for Cork City first-team training at 10am. We'd finish at 12-12.30pm, after a gym session.

I'd grab lunch in the Deanrock Bar in Togher, then report back to school for 2pm.

They worked out a way for me to catch up; if I'd missed English or Maths, I might jump into extra classes in the afternoon where teachers were covering the same topics. School finished at 6pm and then, a few times a week, it was a drive up to Mayfield or down to Ashton School for training on the astroturf with the under-18 or under-21 sides. I wasn't an established first-team player and needed to maintain my connection to the underage teams.

Sometimes I'd go back to school for supervised study, or else head home to get stuck into the books. Next day… the cycle started all over again. Some Friday mornings I'd start off in school but if I was involved with the first-team travelling up to Dublin or Derry, I'd have to get out early.

It was tough work, but I loved it. And I could finally transport myself around, ending the dependency on my parents for lifts.

The previous summer mum and dad had gone on holidays. Sarah was in charge of the house, not that 18-year-old David was going to be told what to do there. So, I made an investment.

A girl I knew… her father was selling a car.

I became the proud owner of a Honda Civic saloon… 96-L-1194, for €500.

I casually mentioned it when dad rang home to see how school was going. Didn't get the thumbs up from the other end of the phone. They were not happy. So, I just needed to sort it before they got back. Dad knew the owner of Canty's Garage on Anglesea Street… I'd been in with him a couple of times.

I got the car into him for a service. Bought the parts off another of dad's buddies, who had a warehouse down near the marina. And I got Canty's to only charge me for the labour… played the card of being just a young lad who needed help.

Then, I went up to some garage in Mayfield and got a big massive exhaust put on the car.

And down to Halfords, where I bought a flip out monitor.

My parents came home, and saw the car was all insured and tidied up. I must have washed it every day for three weeks straight. Eventually I won them over… they could see I was taking care of it.

And they'd a bit more free time instead of driving me around Cork.

ON SUNDAY, NOVEMBER 18, 2007, I played for Cork City in a Youth League Cup final in Turner's Cross.

I'd class it as the most important game I played for the club. We beat Everton 4-0… I was Man of the Match and just ran the midfield. Scored the first, and set up the fourth. Constantly involved.

Physically I was in great shape. The benefits of a full pre-season with the first-team and having people like Colin and Joe pushing me hard was starting to show. I left the pitch that night feeling like I could play another game.

Afterwards, everyone went mad celebrating. I headed up to dad; he was in his usual spot in the middle of the Donie Forde Stand. I was more reserved, felt a bit unfulfilled. We agreed I'd hit a ceiling with the under-18s. I needed more.

Two weeks later, I got a taste of the higher level. Damien Richardson brought me into the senior travelling squad for the FAI Cup final. A wet and windy day at the RDS... Denis Behan hit the only goal in a win over Longford Town.

I was sat in the stand but felt a part of it, and got kitted out by Suits Distributors before the game with the rest of the lads. When Dan Murray lifted the cup, I was on the podium, jumping and roaring with all the lads.

It felt surreal to be there in the middle of the celebrations; a sign that change was coming down the tracks.

I KEPT BOTH education and football going in late-2007 but gradually my energy levels began to drop. Soon I was wrecked most days, struggling to concentrate in class if I'd had a hard training session. I was studying Maths, English, Irish, French, Business, Economics and Accounting. I was up around the 500-point mark in the October exams... then by Christmas it was 450. The decline was slow but noticeable.

Then an offer was put on the table by Cork City... a two-year first-team contract. It had been coming for a couple of months; they wanted to tie me down. I snapped it up and they announced it in January 2008. A month of big calls.

Just before the pre-exams came around, I made another one.

I dropped out of school.

With just four months to go before the Leaving Cert. Dad had noticed it was all starting to pile on top of me.

'What do you want to do?' he asked.

'I want to play football.'

He said, 'Right, that's your decision. But you can have no regrets. Don't turn around later and say you'd wish you'd done something else.'

It still annoys me a bit that I dropped out. *Could I have structured my time better? Should I have asked Cork City about missing some training sessions?* Maybe. But the workload outside of school wasn't sustainable. Leaving school was a decision made for a good reason.

Dad spoke to the people in Bruce; they were very good to deal with and wished me well.

My mother wasn't happy.

She wanted me to finish school and always have the safety net of the Leaving Cert. My grandmother, my mum's mother... she definitely was adamant that I shouldn't drop out. My father said it was my decision… it was my life.

My friends were all young lads like me, wide-eyed to the world. They were thinking this is cool, not having to worry about the Leaving Cert, getting paid to play football. I was on €500 a week, living at home.

I gave my mum €50 a week for board but she did everything for me. I was the only one of my friends who had constant money coming in.

If it didn't work out after a few years at Cork City, I feel I'd have gone back to sit the Leaving again. I'm not sure I'd have drifted around the League of Ireland. I might have looked at college then, focused on a different career and maybe played Munster Senior League on the side.

But that wasn't entering my thinking at the time.

I was so tunnel-visioned.

This is what I want to do.

This is where I'm going.

This is it.

CORK CITY WAS never viewed as a stepping-stone to go to England.

I'd only been in the squad since January and wanted to break into the City first team. That was fuelling my drive, almost making me desperate… get into the side, nail down a position and stay there. My first-team appearances amounted to a couple of games in the Munster Senior Cup and a substitute in a few league games. My focus was on getting more game-time.

Alan Matthews was the club manager by 2008; Damien Richardson had left after the FAI Cup final win. Alan called me in that summer to say a couple of clubs had made enquiries… and Sunderland had made an offer. He was very good to deal with; never stood in my way and kept me updated throughout the whole process.

Did I want to go to England? I was conflicted.

My view was narrow-minded. Living at home with my parents, getting paid good money, hanging around with all my mates… life was great.

Growing up, of course I had dreamed of playing in England but the Cork City situation was a comfort zone that I was probably scared to step out of.

Then, this Sunderland opportunity arose. I didn't have an agent… dad did everything. I was lucky that he looked at the bigger picture. I was living day-to-day, he was thinking of the next 10 years. *What's the career path?*

Cork City was a club in chaos off the pitch in the summer of 2008. I was lucky at my age that I was oblivious to it. For senior players who had families and mortgages, it was different. I was a teenager living at home with my parents. If I was older, I'd have been knocking on doors and looking for answers.

Cork City offered me €3,000 a week to stay. I found it tempting. Thinking… *Why would I want to go to England, when I can get that money to live at home?*

It later emerged players were only getting paid a fraction of their wages so it's hard to believe that offer was serious. Dad makes the point it was lucky I didn't accept it given the uncertainty at the time.

Alan Matthews told me that Roy Keane had been over for a game in Turner's Cross. Alan bumped into him and asked about the transfer.

'Wait and see!'

Typical Roy, keeping his cards close to his chest.

Then Alan called me in one morning, saying the club had accepted a bid and Sunderland would be in touch. Dad always said if the transfer was agreed, we'd sort the contract and I was going. He nudged me in the right direction.

Sunderland booked flights for the two of us to go over; they mentioned to pack enough stuff so I wouldn't have to go home.

Mum was excited about it all. The initial fear factor was gone after dropping out of school. There was a sense that this was a feasible career.

Talk of a move to England had come up before… I went to Aston Villa three or four times as a teenager. Back in Cork after, I was walking around in my Villa gear, thinking… *I'm the bees-knees.*

When I signed for Sunderland, I got more gear than I ever needed and realised you need to earn the right to wear it. Ciaran Clark was on trial with Aston Villa then as well. Years later we became roommates with Ireland.

There was talk Nottingham Forest wanted to sign me at 15… I was over and back all the time. Mum wasn't keen. At that age I was too immature. If I had gone over at that age, I'd have been back living at home by 19, thinking… *What am I going to do with my life?*

WHEN WE FLEW over and met the Sunderland chief executive Margaret Byrne, the negotiations started. A contract was put in front of us and they left the room to give us time to think about it.

I almost wanted dad to make the decision for me.

I'd trust him with my life. He's one of my closest friends. He wasn't motivated by self-interests, he wasn't looking to cash in on a son with sporting talent. His goal was to see me achieve something.

All the previous moves, from Corinthians to Cobh Ramblers… to Cork City; he got those decisions right. He always had a plan. I didn't always see it straightaway but as I settled into each of those teams, I could see he had nailed those decisions and steered me right the whole way.

Now, he might have a Masters in Business… he is a very educated man, but when it comes to football negotiations, he wouldn't be the best.

Sunderland's executives came back into the room after giving us five to 10 minutes to think it all over.

'Maybe we can bump it up a little there,' dad suggested, and threw out a figure.

'No, this is the offer… take it or leave it.'

'Right so, David will sign there,' dad told them.

There was no negotiating. Then we left. We always said it's not about money. If you take care of the work on the pitch, the money follows. It was a good mindset to have.

We checked into the Marriott Hotel that night down by the seaside in Sunderland. He had a flight back first thing in the morning and I was staying.

I was asleep when he left, so he pushed a note under my door. I kept it for years.

This is it.

This is all you've ever wanted.

This is your opportunity.

All the family together enjoying that moment after an Ireland game (top) and mum and Sarah celebrating with me as Hull are promoted to the Premier League.

Mum and Dad with Alanna and Brody.

SATURDAYS

A SATURDAY AFTERNOON home game at three o'clock. One of the most familiar fixtures in English football, one that came to dominate my career.

When I moved to Hull, settled in the area and in the club, I nailed down a Saturday routine and I stuck to it.

Food for the day began with Weetabix in the morning. Later, my future wife Cally introduced pancakes into the mix. She would always have my pre-match meal ready for me at 12... sweet and sour chicken with rice. Same thing every time. I was well looked after, as she'd do all that for me, helping to make sure I was ready to perform. Her help and her presence was something I really appreciated in those days.

I had to be at the stadium at quarter past one.

It's only a 15 minute drive from my house, but I'd leave every time at half twelve. Left nothing to chance... I wasn't going to get caught by traffic or any sort of delay. If it was a weekend with dad was over for a game, he would leave the house at twenty five past twelve... go sit in the car and wait.

At the very start, if Cally was coming to watch the game, she used to come with me at that time as well. That quickly changed. She started going on her own time, and didn't see the point in being there so early, hours before kick-off.

If it was an away game, our schedule was different as we were starting earlier. The Humber View Hotel outside Hull was often the drop off. We'd leave our cars there, hop on the bus that was waiting for us and head off to wherever the game was.

....

I WANT TO arrive by quarter to one... and park up.

I'm en-route too early to come across too many fans... coming off Anlaby Road, while a lot of the fans on matchday make their way down Newlands Avenue and Princes Avenue, going to a bar to get their pints in or grabbing some food... that's where the pre-match atmosphere would be building.

Getting out of my car, there's always a handful of fans with their kids as I make my way into the stadium. They know when the players will be arriving and want to try to catch us for photos or autographs. I don't mind anyone with kids, it's nice to pose with them for a photo and have a few words.

Kids get attached to certain players. It's natural.

They dictate to their fathers. I think of Sergio Aguero approaching Jamie Vardy for his shirt after a Manchester City-Leicester game, just because his son wanted it.

When my son gets a bit older as I bring him to more Hull games, I know he's going to closely follow a couple of players, like the way Keane Lewis-Potter was being idolised last season before his move to Brentford. He'll be looking for that small piece of time with them, that brief interaction which would make his day.

IT'S STRAIGHT DOWN the corridor into the changing room.

The door I enter has a mural on the right, our dominant orange and black colours... with a selection of pictures of some great modern Hull City moments.

The brilliant play-off final goals at Wembley... Dean Windass in 2008... Mohamed Diame in 2016... Phil Brown singing on the pitch after the club avoided relegation from the Premier League.

And there's me celebrating with Paul McShane after his goal in the draw with Cardiff that saw us go up in 2013.

It's lovely to see that, feel a part of that.

We have a squad of over 20 in the first team but only 18 tog out for every game. Friday, we had a tactical session on what shape and formation we were going to take with our opponents in mind. That gives everyone a good idea if they're going to be involved the next day.

We all have the usual spot in the changing room we like, which some of us need.

I walk in the door, and over towards the arch going into the shower area, and sit to the right of that on the bench. Generally, next to Jake Livermore and Tom Huddlestone. On the other side of the arch is Curtis Davies.

I chat with the kitmen, who are all waiting... as players file in... in ones and twos.

Some lads land in and get stripped, putting on their kit straightaway. I've seen it happen on a few occasions... not many, but there is a lad who gets changed and ultimately he's not in the squad for the game. That's a bit awkward.

The kitman puts out the kit for every member of the squad.

Team announcements can vary. Sometimes it's on a Thursday or Friday... sometimes on the Saturday when we arrived to the stadium.

I never mind not knowing until a couple of hours before a game.

When I played for Ireland there was a huge debate over Martin O'Neill's style of just telling us the team not long before kick-off. I've seen it happen where a team is announced on a Thursday before a Saturday afternoon game and that session is awful because the lads who aren't in the team are annoyed.

A Friday announcement can have a similar reaction. Often the best thing is to announce it on the Saturday... and keep everybody on their toes.

I WAIT, ALWAYS... for the manager to speak before getting changed into my gear.

Quarter past one is the designated cut-off time for everyone to be here. But there's always a few who come in the door at 1.14pm. Curtis is a prime example.

He is never late, but always just leaves it to the last 30 seconds. I'm looking at the clock, thinking... *he's going to be late.* Then he appears.

If the game's on TV, a couple of lads are brought down for an interview.

The manager is not going to come in until half past one.

Everyone will be settled by then. The projector turned on... the screen pulled down, and he will go through the starting eleven... what he wants us to do. From that moment on, it is time to get the game face on.

Initially, after announcing the team, the manager speaks for about 10 minutes tops. Then it's about us, the players... getting ourselves right , seeing the medics if needed. I always have to do some work on my knee right... treatment with the physio Rob Price, pre-activation work to get the muscles in my leg going,

I pop into a small room next to the changing room and hop on one of the spinning bikes. There's be a few lads in there doing exercises... the strength and conditioning coach is in there as well overseeing things.

That is a good time to nail down set piece instructions as well. I learned from Roy Keane years ago, that it's not enough to just know what you're doing on a corner or free-kick... you need to know what two or three people are doing. Taking on the information of numerous roles makes it a lot easier when we get out onto the pitch.

Good communication and clear understanding.

TWENTY PAST TWO, we're out on the pitch.

Forty minutes before kick-off... enough time to get set. There is a small bit of downtime before we head out... talking away to lads, reading the match programme. At quarter past two, the sports scientist shouts out, 'FIVE MINUTES!'

They're in charge of the warm-up.

Timing and sticking to the schedule is key.

We go out the tunnel and turn to our right to warm up in front of the South Stand. The away fans are at the opposite end, in a corner that stretches from the North Stand into the East Stand... right next to a hardcore group of Hull City fans in the East Stand.

Warm-up will usually be 20-25 minutes.

There are plenty of fans in at this stage, the ground gradually starting to build up, but there's still loads of latecomers. It's only when we're in the tunnel, five to 10 minutes before the game starts, that we'll really sense the noise and buzz around the place.

We're back into the changing room at 20 to three.

The manager is in his room with his staff.

He gives a few last messages.

Players head to the toilet.

Make sure boots are tied... shinpads, tape done on the socks.

One last glance at the set pieces. A final instruction from the manager.

Players are talking... everyone is getting fired up.

An alarm goes off to signal it's eight minutes to kick off... we're out the door... out from the tunnel into the light, emerging onto the pitch... the noise rolling around the stadium as the fans arrive at full voice.

It's three o'clock... the whistle sounds.

Time to get to work, chase that win... three precious league points.

....

I'D USUALLY BE on the road home from the stadium by six o'clock.

You might have media duties to fulfil if you'd played well. Some lads rush out to do them, others shower and change first... gather their thoughts before facing the microphones. If you do them fresh after the game, emotions can come into it.

The time Ireland got hammered by Denmark, 5-1... James McClean did an interview he should never have done. He was too raw.

People applauded him for speaking straight from the heart, but that's a time when you need to settle your emotions.

The Man of the Match often has to go up and see some of the corporate figures associated with the club... have a few words, chat about the match. After a win and you get that bottle of champagne, you're running up the steps to the corporate boxes.

Life is great.

But if you lose and have to go up, it's a chore... questions to face about the defeat, and you've no interest in those discussions. All part and parcel of a professional football life!

I MISS THAT buzz on a Saturday.

Getting up, starting the preparations for the game and making sure everything is right. The simple things. Arriving at the stadium, the camaraderie with the lads in the dressing-room.

Chit-chatting... having a laugh. The same with the buzz after a good result... and we're all going out together for a few drinks afterwards.

Those are the things I miss about life as a footballer

Sunderland

I SAUNTERED INTO the changing room for the first day of training with the Sunderland reserves before the 2008-09 season started. In my own head, I was the Cork lad coming over, miles ahead of the rest. *This group of fellas will be no problem.*

Jordan Henderson and Jack Colback were there on day one.

Jamie Chandler too, a highly-rated England youth international at the time. I remember the goalkeeper Trevor Carson, and the striker Martyn Waghorn.

And they were all miles ahead of me. That first day I was way off the pace. I walked into a squad of 22 players, but take out the couple of goalkeepers and I was ranked 19 out of 20.

All these fellas were technically excellent.

The standard was ridiculous.

THE BEST THING that had happened to me was training with the Cork City first-team, with Colin, Gareth and Joe showing me the way. Understanding the need to knuckle down was nothing new. I was able to properly assess the situation, then enjoy the challenge. You get more comfortable in the group and your personality starts to shine in training.

It just takes time. I was nervous after that first session though. They were competitive too... they weren't going to let some Irish lad come over and take their position. I had made my Sunderland debut back home in Turner's Cross in a friendly against Cobh Ramblers that had been pre-arranged.

When I had first flown to Sunderland, I didn't bring much stuff. My dad just threw a lot of clothes into the bag and gave it to me after that friendly. He didn't want me coming home regularly; his focus was on getting me settled over there and not thinking about family or buddies around Cork.

IT WASN'T UNTIL Christmas that I came back home and that proved disastrous in a way. We finished up our reserve league on December 18, and were let off until January 1. But when I was home, the club rang; they wanted myself and Jordan to go training with the first-team. It was grand for Jordan, he was nearby.

I was in another country.

Dad was saying to get on a flight and get back over there. But they wanted us there the following morning. Jordan went in and trained; I couldn't make it over. That Christmas, dad was really annoyed that I was around the house. He felt I should have stayed, toughed it out on my own and be ready if a chance came up.

He was big on the idea of me not coming home regularly. He'd done enough research to see young fellas got homesick, and use to go home all the time. His thinking was… if he could get me settled over in England, not thinking about family or my buddies, I would have a better chance of making a proper go of it.

It was never an issue again. I got in around the first-team afterwards, so my Christmas breaks were never as long again.

The first morning after dad had left, I went into training. After that finished, I was back in the hotel by early afternoon. *How would I fill my days?* The focus was getting somewhere to stay and getting a car.

The club helped find me an apartment. Once I got the initial help, I was off on my own. I was completely lost, a 19-year-old in a new city in the north of England. I got the apartment and rang my mother to check what I needed. Microwave, kettle, cutlery… kitchen essentials.

'Have you got a bed?'

No, I didn't have a bed, and had to go get one.

I got organised… sorted a TV, chased up Sky and an internet connection. A big culture shock. Mum talked me through everything… but I'd never cooked in my life.

'Mum, what food do I need?'

'Right, get yourself some chicken, put it in the freezer. Take it out and defrost it… put it in the oven and you're sorted.'

I listened closely. The problem was I didn't defrost the chicken properly. I was ill for about four days; I'll never forget it.

Then I came across Nandos. That sorted me.

I WASN'T THE only Cork young lad at the club. Conor Hourihane from Bandon was there before me, and John Egan from Bishopstown joined the following year in 2009. There was only a few years between us in age so we got on well.

The day I arrived, Conor came over and introduced himself. It was a nice touch; he'd played with Douglas Hall, who were local rivals of Corinthians.

A couple years previously, when I used to train in Mayfield for Cork City teams, there was an Irish emerging talent squad based there that Colin O'Brien ran. Conor was the great prospect that a lot of people talked about.

Himself and John both made it to the Premier League, but only after leaving Sunderland and scrapping to show the fight they had in them. Conor had a long road playing at lower levels, starting from scratch with Plymouth and building himself up. I'd give them huge credit for that.

I always want to see Cork lads succeeding, and there's a layer of responsibility I always felt in keeping an eye out for them, having a word with coaches as to how they're going. Kevin Ball used to always rave about John at Sunderland.

John is a remarkable man, I've so much time for him. He's very adaptable, and has a great work ethic. It took him until the age of 27 to reach the Premier League, but I had no fear of him when he got there.

In 2012, John had a bad leg break, while out on loan at Bradford. I drove down to visit him in hospital after. Despite the pain, he was still positive and upbeat. I was so happy to see him later make it to the Premier League with Sheffield United; the same when Conor did it with Aston Villa.

There's that sense of brotherhood in English football amongst the Irish crew; we've all moved over and we're all trying to make it. With John and Conor, there was that extra element in we'd all grown up in Cork.

I think I had the easier road of the three of us. That may sound strange with my knee injuries but I didn't have to dive down to the lower leagues as a young player. You can get pigeon-holed. If you drop down to League One, you can be stuck there… and the Premier League seems a million miles away.

I HAD MY own Irish support network when I started at Sunderland… Graham Kavanagh, Paul McShane, Andy Reid, Daryl Murphy, Roy O'Donovan and Liam Miller. They all looked out for me. I was at the club a month and a group of them took me out for a night in Newcastle. They were all brilliant.

Andy Reid was probably the hardest on me. He had standards and would be on a young player's case… 24/7, and didn't want anyone to slack off. We had a run-in one day at training. Reidy had fantastic skill with a beautiful left foot. I passed him the ball, and he carved open the defence with this great pass and we got in for a goal.

I shouted over, 'Great ball, son!' He absolutely flipped at me.

'Who are you calling son?'

I was gobsmacked he went after me. I was trying to compliment him; I understood later that he took it differently, seeing me belittling him.

There was another 10 minutes of training left. We were walking in after and I was chatting to Jordan about what happened. His view was not to be bullied by him.

Then big Murph came over.

'I wouldn't take that if it were me. You can't let him speak to you like that.'

He was winding me up… and was over to Reidy doing the exact same thing. 'This young kid from Cork is mugging you off. You really going to take it?'

We'd a gym session after it, and Reidy came storming in. I gave it back to him; we were roaring at each other. There were no punches thrown, we both just lost the head. I made sure not to call him son again.

But those Irish lads were very good.

Graham Kavanagh was a tough Dubliner, a good honest pro. He showed me the ropes before he then moved on to Carlisle. They all looked out for me. They'd all been down the road of coming over from Ireland to England, and knew it could be tricky. Just all good, decent lads… no major egos. Dwight Yorke wasn't part of that group but he was a brilliant figure for the younger lads, always wanting to help us.

To us he had the fame; a decade on from winning the treble with Man United, we were all a bit starstruck by him. He'd talk to us and point out little things we needed to work on… focusing on our passing, our positioning when receiving the ball. He'd this typical West Indies personality; very relaxed and chilled, nothing really bothered him.

We played a game once against a local team called Consett. I was midfield with Yorkie; one of those surreal days when I'm staring at him on the pitch for a second and getting my head around this situation.

ALL THE IRISH lads were great, but they were a good few years older. And they had their own families to focus on. I was living in this weird bubble.

It would have been different if I was a 15-year-old thrown into that environment, trying to keep the homesickness at bay. I found Sunderland similar in size and scale to Cork; and the same working-class city where people are highly passionate about their sport.

My buddies used to come over every second week, different lads. One weekend when I got into the first-team, four of them landed. We were playing a game on the Saturday, and the lads went out on the Friday night. I told them going out to let themselves back into my house later – I'd moved from the apartment by then – just not to wake me up.

But they got into a scrap in the middle of Sunderland and one of them had his jaw broken. The following morning, I was getting up, preparing for the game and your man has strapping on his jaw… he's black and blue.

Suddenly, I'm dealing with this, instead of preparing for a game.

I was young and naive. As I got older, I didn't allow such a scenario to occur; I got more selfish about my preparation before games.

I'M JUST OVER a year older than Jordan Henderson.

When I signed, there was a little pre-season tournament down the coast in Hartlepool. James McCarthy was playing for Hamilton in it… people were raving about this kid. My registration hadn't gone through so I wasn't allowed play. Jordan had a quad injury.

So, we were told, 'When the game is on, you two go and sit behind the dugout'.

We just got chatting and struck up a friendship. Jordan was shy and reserved, in this bubble of wanting to be a footballer, determined not to let any other distractions interfere with that. Our relationship evolved over time; we started doing stuff together outside of training and matches.

We laugh about it now, but I used to ring Jordan in the evenings.

'What are you up to… will we go to Nandos… to the cinema after?'

'I can't, I don't have the money for it.'

'Ah come on, I'll pay for you.'

We were on different contracts, myself and the future Liverpool captain… and Premier League and Champions League winner. But I knew him when he needed a dig out for chicken and chips for his dinner, some money for popcorn and a film ticket after. We joked about those times when he got the big move to Liverpool. Later Jordan bought the Audi off me, and Conor Hourihane bought it off Jordan. That car did the rounds. I became very good friends with his crew from school, who I'd still be friends with now.

We'd play with the reserves on a Tuesday or Wednesday night. Jordan never went out or drank but I'd go out at times with his mates, who were all in university.

That's how we became friends and over a decade on we're still close.

Jordan's mentality was at a really high level from day one. He was always a really good footballer but he has developed so much there. Working with top managers like Kenny Dalglish, Brendan Rodgers and Jurgen Klopp would have all brought him on in turn, but his own attitude would have played a big part as well. He drives himself forward all the time. I still find it fascinating that he is captain of Liverpool.

That wasn't a role I'd have seen him taking on in the early days at Sunderland. He was a quiet lad… would only ever speak up if something really had to be said.

I suppose his work as a captain was around the way he conducted himself, the way he trained, the way he prepared, looked after himself and recovered. He was a manager's dream in his outlook. The type of man you'd want your daughter to bring home. He's matured over the years when given that added responsibility… growing and learning how to lead that group. At times it may have seemed an easy choice for Jurgen Klopp to take that armband off him but you can see how much he values and respects him.

I always find it interesting that in the games where Jordan doesn't start for Liverpool and then comes on, how quickly they give him the armband. He's been the leader when Liverpool have won the biggest prize in English football and the biggest prize in European football. He's the only Englishman to have lifted the Premier League, the Champions League, the Super Cup and the Club World

Cup. That's history-making stuff.

When football returned after the first Covid-lockdown in 2020 and fans weren't allowed at games, it was interesting how you could always hear him when Liverpool were playing. His high squeaky voice, moaning and groaning at his teammates for 90 minutes. But they all respond to him.

That shows what they think of him.

THERE WAS NO major meet and greet with Roy Keane when I signed for Sunderland. I do remember seeing him early on in my first week. It had always been drilled into me to be first for training. Coaches take notice of that. It was a Friday morning… I arrived and Roy was there.

'Morning Roy!'

I was oblivious to the chain of command in soccer. You do not call a manager by his first name. He replied, 'Morning!'

He didn't go through me, but there was enough of a lingering look to suggest I'd get a pass this once, but in future… it was 'Gaffer' and nothing else.

My first real experience of Roy's attitude was when we played Gateshead away in a pre-season friendly with the reserves. I knew nothing about Gateshead; it was a half-hour from Sunderland; they were playing in the Conference North at the time. We played the game and lost 2-0.

Roy was due to go back to Manchester but decided to stay and watch the game with his staff. The plan was for everybody to leave from the ground after. But after we got beaten the message came through that all the players were to report to the training ground. The manager wanted to speak to us.

In the Academy of Light, there was a big TV room upstairs, which had couches scattered around the large screen. We were waiting for Roy.

He came up and ordered everyone to stand up.

We stood in a circle around him. It was my first eye-opener of what life in England was about. He spoke about the performance of the team and hammered into a lot of people. We had a mix of senior professionals playing with us younger lads. Graham Kavanagh got a fair bit of stick.

Roy had a cut off Jordan, asking him did he think he was good enough to play for the first-team. Jordan looked him straight in the eye.

'Yeah, I do!'

I'd been at Sunderland only a week or so, but he turned to look at me.

'Just because you've only just signed, don't think you can get away with that. This is serious… you need to buck yourself up.'

It was an insight to his level of expectations.

If anyone thought it was a run of the mill pre-season friendly, they were wrong. Some lads crumbled under that pressure. I felt this was what it was all about; hearing from a manager who was honest and open. My dad would have had similar conversations where he'd point out flaws in my performances.

That day flicked a switch in my head about how he was such a successful captain for Manchester United and why he was arguably the best player Ireland has ever produced. He had high standards that needed to be met. Over the years I've got to know him and had conversations with him.

He has never once claimed he was a fantastic player. He just worked extremely hard and did everything to get the best out of himself.

We had all played awful in the game, but Jordan made his Premier League debut a couple of months later against Chelsea. The two of us were on the bench; Jordan was brought on at half-time. Roy admired that Jordan believed in himself and that he wasn't going to shy away from a challenge.

When he gave it to me with both barrels after that Gateshead game, I just replied, 'Okay.'

I had heard what he had to say.

I was going to look to push on now.

AT THE SUNDERLAND training ground, there was a whiteboard on the wall outside the doctor's office, between the changing rooms for the first-team and the reserve team. I checked it every morning to see the training squads for that day.

It wasn't unusual to go with the first-team, but generally it was if they needed cover due to injuries. Thursday was the important day. That's when tactical work is done for that weekend's game.

Make the cut then and it's a sign you're closer to the first-team squad.

The start of the 2008-09 season was about adjusting to life with Sunderland. After 10 games, November began with a trip to Chelsea.

For the Thursday session before that match, myself, Jordan and Martyn Waghorn were on the first-team list on the whiteboard. Big progress. On the Friday, the squad list for the game went up.

I was heading to Stamford Bridge.

Welcome to the Premier League; private flight to London that evening, coach waiting on arrival, whisked straight to the team hotel. From where I had been a few months before with Cork City, this was a world apart.

I wasn't fazed about potentially playing against one of the best sides in the country. But I was worried about something.

The night before the game was time for my initiation song.

We all had our own rooms, and directly across the hall from me was Anton Ferdinand. Before dinner he was on FaceTime to Rio and saying, 'We've got this young kid here from Ireland…he's got to go sing for us'.

Rio was shouting not to forget any words. It was all good-natured but it wasn't helping me relax.

After dinner myself, Jordan and Martyn had to sing as the new lads. They did a duet of a Ne-Yo song… I went my own way. I walked into the meeting room and stepped up on a chair. Everyone's roaring and banging the tables.

I planned to sing *The Streets of New York* by The Wolfe Tones… knew the words inside out. I got through the first three lines… and then my mind went blank.

Nothing.

The lads all tore strips off me. And then Andy Reid saved the day. He's a great man for a song; he just stood up and joined in with me. Daryl Murphy did the same. It was awful but they got me through it.

I sat down, sweat dripping off me.

By then Roy and the rest of the coaches had come down. Someone turned to Roy.

'Meyler's just sang.'

'Ohhhhh… has he?' Roy turned to me.

'Get back up there and sing again, so we can see it this time!'

If ever there was a time that my soul left my body, that was it. Roy saw how I had frozen; he just laughed and walked off.

CHELSEA PICKED A team full of stars.

Petr Cech, Alex, John Terry, Ashley Cole, José Bosingwa, John Obi Mikel, Frank Lampard, Joe Cole, Deco, Florent Malouda… Nicolas Anelka.

This was the big time and I loved the thought of going up against these fellas. I spent the 90 minutes on the bench watching on. Martyn started up front and Jordan came on at half-time for his debut.

The game was an eye-opener. We lost 5-0.

Nicolas Anelka was outstanding; he scored a hat-trick and won the Golden Boot that season. I always found him a fascinating character; he seemed to have a real edge to him. I hadn't played but still found it a huge experience. I wanted to become a regular in the first-team squad.

Then, a month later, Roy Keane left the club.

IT WAS A Thursday morning in early December, two days before playing Manchester United, when word spread around the club that he'd left.

Footballers must be selfish when assessing the situation. I was only in the door a few months. *Where did I stand?* Roy had signed me and must have thought I was half-decent. I was having a sniff around the first-team, things were going positively and then, suddenly… he was gone. I didn't see it coming.

A 4-1 loss to Bolton the previous Saturday had left us in the relegation zone. A fifth defeat in six games. That form would suggest a manager was in trouble but I was young and naive. As I got older, I realised football is a tough business. There is no loyalty; it's rare people leave of their own accord.

I found it a difficult time.

A fella who had put faith in me was gone. I wanted to play for Roy and I didn't get that opportunity properly until later in my career with Ireland. I didn't even have his phone number at the time to contact him and say I appreciated what he'd done.

Ricky Sbragia took over until the end of the season, a Scottish coach who had been at the club for a while. But Ricky's focus wasn't on young lads, it was about experience. He needed to survive a relegation battle and did that, despite only winning once in the last 13 games. Our North-East neighbours Newcastle and Middlesbrough went down.

That Chelsea trip was my one first-team experience… I kept playing with the reserves. We won the North League and lost to Aston Villa, winners of the South League, 3-1 in a play-off.

I turned 20 that May, and had a season in England under my belt, but things felt uncertain. It was all well and good having a contract, but I couldn't just sit there for a couple of years, take the money and head home.

I needed to play and prove myself.

Ricky left at the end of the season. In June, the new manager arrived.

THIS WAS THE beginning of my time in football with Steve Bruce.

Myself and dad chatted in the summer of 2009 before I went back to Sunderland for pre-season. We agreed this was a crucial time. I had to start impressing if I wanted to make that breakthrough. I was always naturally fit; prided myself on that.

You could pick technical faults in my game but when it came to running, I was convinced no one would beat me.

We started in July doing a lot of energy-sapping running sessions, and I was like a machine. We used a 1km track for interval running, doing a drill that would last 25 minutes with six stations… jog for so long, then the call came to go flat-out.

My goal was to stand out and I did that.

I got the call-up for the pre-season tour to Portugal. It went well. We went on to Amsterdam, playing in a mini-tournament against Benfica, Atletico Madrid and Ajax. My parents were flying in to watch the games. Steve Bruce let me know I was in the picture to play.

I was excited. Then a setback. In training, I got the ball, went to fire a one-two around Phil Bardsley and he dived in, ripping all my ankle ligaments.

Out for six weeks.

The lads went to Amsterdam. I flew back to Sunderland on my own. It was my first experience of the mental grind of injury recovery. Bruce rang with a simple message… 'Get your ankle sorted and you'll be fine'.

That spurred me on. I worked with the physio Dave Binningsley; we'd later become very close with my two serious knee injuries.

Before the start of the season, the Sunderland coaches were concerned I'd missed a good chunk of training. I was pushing and threw myself into training. Then I got clattered into my left ankle. Another six weeks out… back to injury rehab.

As the weeks passed, I needed a proper game to test my ankle. There was one arranged behind closed doors with our reserves against Doncaster Rovers. It looked a nothing game but it proved critical for me in winning the trust of Bruce. About half hour in, one of our young lads got cleaned out. I was one of the oldest Sunderland players and didn't like the tackle.

I had a pop off the lad who went in, before the referee came over to calm things down.

THERE IS A beauty to tackling.

People think you just hurl your body at it but you have to catch someone at precisely the right time. The ball came to that same Doncaster lad.

He received it on the backfoot.

I came like a train; cleaned him and the ball. A perfect tackle.

The ref stopped the game, because the lad jumped up and grabbed me by the neck… handbags stuff. The ref wanted to put us both off; he wasn't happy, this was meant to be low-key. Next thing I see Steve walking onto the pitch and he puts his arm around me. We walked off and they brought on a sub.

'Do a five-minute jog around the pitch,' Bruce told me.

'Go for an ice bath and cool off.' I wondered was I in trouble since the manager had got involved. But I'd built up a good rapport with Dave. He gave me the heads up on how Bruce had reacted to the tackle.

'He'll do for me!' Bruce had said. 'You can't put the fight in someone, but you can control it.' That was a stepping-stone for me to get into the first-team.

It didn't mean instant progression. I was in my dad's ear that maybe I needed to go on loan. But by Christmas, the Sunderland squad was hit hard by injuries. I wasn't involved for the 1-1 draw with Everton on December 26. Two days later we were away to Blackburn.

This time I was in. All my family were over for the game at Ewood Park. I tuned in that morning…. breakfast, walk, pre-match food… team meeting. I was sitting with Michael Liddle, an Ireland under-21 teammate, as the team was put up on the big screen.

I immediately looked at the subs list.

Hadn't made it.

I was giving out to Michael... and then he nudged me... 'Look... you're starting!'

I looked again.

David Meyler midfield with Lorik Cana and Jordan Henderson. A breakthrough at last. We got to the stadium and Bruce marched over during the warm-up.

'Just keep it simple. Don't try any Hollywood passes.

'Win the ball back... lay it off... go again!'

IT ALL FELT frantic as the game started.

After a few minutes, I ran onto a ball about 30 yards out, had a crack and it flew over the bar. Whatever nerves I had were now gone. I was up for it.

I charged into Morten Gamst Pedersen in midfield. Steven Nzonzi and Keith Andrews squared up to me. A yellow card to mark my debut.

All the details are clear in my mind.

All four goals arrived in a 25-minute period in the second-half... Darren Bent put us ahead twice, Pedersen and El- Hadji Diouf equalised. Steve Bruce versus Sam Allardyce on the touchline... a draw after a mid-table scrap.

That day was a good insight into a big theme in Sunderland's season, the goalscoring of Darren Bent. The previous August he had signed for a club record fee of £10 million. If there was pressure because of that price, it didn't affect him. He was an unbelievable finisher and worked on it relentlessly every day in training.

Of the people I played with, he was similar to Robbie Keane. Obsessed with scoring goals. Benty might do nothing all game but you knew if he got a chance that he'd score. In his London twang, he'd say he wasn't there to run the channels or close people down. You hear about strikers who play the width of the box... that was Darren Bent.

He finished the season with 24 goals in the Premier League, third top scorer behind Didier Drogba and Wayne Rooney.

Most people remember his famous 'beach ball' goal against Liverpool, but another one sticks out in my mind.

Third last game of the season was away to Hull. Early on, I won the ball and moved it wide to Alan Hutton. He launched in a cross, Kenwyne Jones headed it back… and Benty sticks it in the net. We were the first two running off in celebration, hugging each other… and then he turned to me.

'Bruv, you've just helped pay for my Ferrari!'

It was his 24th league goal but, more importantly, it was his 25th overall for the season. He had a bonus in his contract if he hit that milestone, and had ordered himself a Ferrari as a reward. We all knew his value to the squad. Bruce reminded us in January when we lost 2-0 to Everton and he hit the roof after.

'If it wasn't for him down there, we'd be in big trouble!' he roared while pointing at Benty.

He knew how to score goals and that's not an easy trait. A wonderful player to have in your team.

I was all ears anytime I was in the company of Roy Keane who signed me for Sunderland (here we are together on Ireland duty), but when he was replaced by Steve Bruce I found myself a second 'father' figure.

MY FOOTBALL HOME

THE NAME HAS changed but the site is the same on Walton Street, just off Anlaby Road in Hull.

This is now the stadium that I have the greatest affiliation for in the world. I joined the club a decade after they moved from Boothferry Park. The KC Stadium is where I started playing, then it became the KCOM Stadium in my final years with Hull and now it's the MKM Stadium where I go to watch the team play, bringing my kids along to introduce them as new supporters.

For everyone growing up who is into sport, stadiums are special places.

Back in Cork, Turner's Cross was the big football stadium to go to matches or play schoolboys games in. With my gaelic games background, Páirc Uí Chaoimh had a huge status. Then nationally for football, Lansdowne Road in Dublin was the focus, or the Aviva Stadium... after it was redeveloped and where I got to play with the Ireland senior team.

BUT IT IS a place in east Yorkshire that is the location for some of my best experiences.

My first memory of the stadium is coming here to play with Sunderland near the end of the season in April 2010. Darren Bent scored early on, we won 1-0 and Hull were relegated soon after.

That was a taste as an away player, but a few years later it became my football home. So many memories jump out.

The crazy game that sealed promotion in 2013... I won a penalty near the end of that draw with Cardiff and the fans rushed on from the South Stand before we'd to order them off the pitch.

Then, later that year, the win over Liverpool... on the left-hand side of the penalty box in front of the South Stand, managing to control my shot and finding the bottom corner of the net.

The Sunderland game in 2014... that brilliant win for us in the FA Cup quarter-final, a perfect day when we won 3-0 and knew we were all heading to Wembley as a club.

Playing here against Manchester United when I scored in a defeat, Wayne Rooney hitting that outrageous volley for them.

Taking on the same team in a league cup semi-final... the second leg, where we were chasing them down to try to get a comeback, a midweek night when the crowd were roaring us on.

Facing Manchester City, the reigning league champions in the early stages of the 2013-14 seasons... Edin Dzeko putting a couple of really good goals past us.

The opportunities to test yourself against the best.

THE STADIUM SOLD out regularly in those seasons we were in the Premier League. It had the glamour, and those games drew the crowds when the top teams were in town. I'm not sure it was an intimidating place for away sides to come to, but my take is that it's really only the games away to the big six that are intimidating. Those are the venues where the crowd can get inside a player's head, the atmosphere piling on the pressure.

Outside of that? I don't know if that fear factor exists for players.

Don't get me wrong, there are stadiums that are difficult places to play in but they don't have to be overwhelming. There are those traditional English football clubs who have been at the heart of the Premier League. Everton for example, I loved playing at Goodison Park. A hard place to get a result but a tight city stadium, that feel of the fans breathing down your neck as they were so close to the pitch, that was something I fed off and wanted to experience.

Crystal Palace was the same at Selhurst Park, that sort of cauldron feel to the ground.

The Hull fans could make a serious noise when the place was full. I often think you have to give the fans something to cheer about. You can't just automatically expect them to be bouncing from the opening minutes.

I think one of the reasons I was appreciated at Hull was how hard I worked on the pitch. You could pick faults at times in my passing, or my finishing or other technical qualities. But no one ever got at me for not putting it in. If I played an hour, 75 minutes, 15 off the bench or the full 90 plus, I gave everything I had for that period of time I was on the pitch.

Again, I credit that to my background. The gaelic games upbringing I had, the general values my dad helped instil in me when it came to sport. You have to buy into what it's about. Giving the required level of effort is non-negotiable.

I look at Seamus Coleman and James McClean, friends I've played alongside for Ireland, still doing their stuff at Everton and Wigan. They play with pride. Mistakes may happen but their passion, their emotion, their commitment to the cause can never be questioned.

Those are really good and important qualities in a footballer. That passion can spill over at times, so you need to keep it in check.

....

THE FEELING OF scoring a goal in a Hull home game was a pure rush of joy and adrenaline. That goal by the South Stand saw a few memorable ones.

The FA Cup quarter-final against Sunderland, running the length of the pitch, getting to the ball ahead of Cattermole... racing in and keeping my head to finish with my left foot. Listening to the crowd that day, the nervousness at being ahead 1-0, then the sense of rising anticipation as I get clear... the shouts get louder as I get closer to the goal, and then that eruption of noise when the ball is in the net.

That realisation we're on the way to Wembley. Matty Fryatt got the third goal five minutes later. That second-half was an amazing buzz.

It's 20 years since Hull City left Boothferry Park and moved to this stadium, to this part of the town. To have been involved for the years that saw some of the club's greatest moments on this pitch, is a genuine privilege. I define a playing career as one where can you look back on moments and be proud to talk about them!

Do other people want to engage in those recollections as well? I feel I have that from my time at Hull. Not just what we achieved in results, but the connection that was built between the players and the club and the fans.

I WAS FORTUNATE during that 2020-21 season to get asked to co-commentate for the club media on some of their games. At a time when the doors were closed to fans during the pandemic, it was a privilege to be allowed in to watch a game of football. It was all part of the deal the EFL made at the time that every club would livestream their games. The fans had to stay at home, but at least they could still watch on.

During that time you cherish those moments a lot more. It was really nice of Hull as a club to approach me and allow me to do that. I jumped at the opportunity when it came up. One day I headed up to Sunderland to do commentary work when they were playing Hull. It was September 2020, a League Cup game that Hull won on penalties.

That was a surreal experience, driving up the motorway with so little traffic and into an almost empty stadium that I knew so well. It summed up the weird times... the players' voices clearly heard with no fans there to roar them on.

I'm not a regular at every home game, but I go now and then to the MKM Stadium. Maybe 10-12 times last season in the Championship. Different things crop up like family plans on a Saturday, or if I'm caught doing some media work for the radio station Newstalk in Ireland. I like going to games but there's lot of variables about it fitting into whatever's on in my weekend.

In mid-April 2022, I went to see Hull play at home to Cardiff. It was the first time the four of us as a family had gone to a game. It was great to see all the security guards, girls at reception, a few people upstairs. Really nice to chat away to them.

Cally sent my dad some photos of the kids at the game... I was able to bring Alanna and Brody straight down to the pitch to meet the mascots, Amber and Roary, and get pictures with them. Dad was saying how he missed going to the games there. And Cally loved getting to meet so many people that we hadn't seen in years.

MY DAD HAD come to nearly every game, and he got to know people.

They would still come up to me in the crowd and say how's your dad, because they'd have been at home and away games, they'd see him sitting down... and he'd made connections with them.

Hull won that game against Cardiff 2-1. After six home defeats in-a-row, they scored two early goals inside the opening 11 minutes from Allahyar Sayyadmanesh and Lewie Coyle.

Those goals created a real buzz around the stadium. Cardiff got a late goal but Hull held on for the victory.

It had been a difficult season at times in the Championship but now near the end of the season, there were no more relegation worries to be concerned about.

Being back at the stadium that day, sitting in the stand with my family was a new chapter in my relationship with Hull City.

It still felt good to be there.

6

Welcome to Hull

I FLEW TO Marbella at the end of the 2012-13 season. I had a few days to kill before reporting for Ireland duty, so myself and Kelogs – my best friend Peter Kelleher – took off to the sun.

We were in a restaurant one day when the Championship play-off semi-final came on TV… Watford against Leicester. The end of the game was absolutely wild. Anthony Knockaert missed a penalty for Leicester in injury-time… Watford went straight downfield and Troy Deeney scored the winner to send them to Wembley.

Pitch invasion… pure mayhem!

Looking at that madness, I was glad to be watching on. The previous week had been crazy enough…. last day league drama. It's the outcome TV executives and viewers are craving. Late goals, permutations, fans smiling and in tears. The hype machine is stirred into overdrive as the promotion and relegation storylines play out.

The final day with Hull City that year packed in the type of drama that I'm not sure will be surpassed. We should have had a relaxing end to the season, but we won none of our last four games. We took over 5,000 fans to Barnsley with plans for a promotion party and lost 2-0 to a team fighting relegation.

It came down to the last Saturday afternoon.

We were second and playing Cardiff, a point ahead of Watford who faced Leeds.

Half-time.

We're drawing 0-0.

Watford were drawing 1-1.

And the madness kicked in.

My good friend Frazier Campbell put Cardiff ahead; it looked like we were bottling it. Then our German striker Nick Proschwitz made it 1-1.

Five minutes later Paul McShane put us in front.

Deep into injury-time, we were hanging on to that lead, when they went down to 10 men. A couple of minutes later, I got ahead of the defender in the box and… FOUL!

Penalty!

Some fans thought the referee has blown for full-time and raced onto the pitch… it took a few minutes to clear them off before Proschwitz struck the penalty.

SAVED!

Cardiff booted the rebound down the pitch and won a throw-in. Aron Gunnarsson has a ridiculous long throw; he hurt England with Iceland in Euro 2016, and this time he hurled it into our box.

Goalmouth scramble!

HANDBALL… and Cardiff got a 95th minute penalty. Nicky Maynard scored. 2-2.

Full-time.

Our heads were melted; screaming for the Watford scoreline, then discovering there'd been a big delay at Vicarage Road. Watford had to change their goalkeeper just before the game, then the replacement went off injured and they'd to bring in a youngster.

Dream stuff for Sky Sports.

They whack a camera into the KC Stadium tunnel where our players have all raced in to watch the Watford-Leeds game. Lads are screaming for it to be over… I had stayed in the changing room with the staff until the final whistle sounded, then I had sprinted out to join my dad and Kelogs.

It's a long wait. Fifteen minutes for the result. The entire stadium is on edge.

A Watford goal and we're in trouble.

Then the roar came… an eruption of noise as the news filtered through. Leeds had scored, Ross McCormack chipping the goalkeeper. Soon it's confirmed. We're promoted... just as Steve Bruce had promised the previous November when he rang and asked me to come to Hull.

We'd nothing planned for after that game, the celebrations were all completely off the cuff. When we left the stadium, we went down to Newland Avenue and into a bar. I remember I bought everyone in there a drink, got the staff to give us crates of Desperados bottled beer and just started handing them out to people.

That whole experience was just crazy, but what made it so special was I was with dad when this rollercoaster of a day came to a halt. We were hugging in the stadium afterwards and there were tears of joy as we realised we were heading to the Premier League.

It was all we'd ever wanted, and we were together when it happened.

THE HULL CITY squad I joined was filled with players that had enjoyed brief tastes of Premier League football. They wanted that experience regularly. It was the unspoken goal driving us all on.

The squad was filled with strong characters and they formed a tight-knit bunch. Paul McShane and Robbie Brady both lived in James Chester's house. That was the group I slotted into.

Every Friday before a home game, a group of us would hang out at Chester's house. Paul McShane would cook dinner. Usually it was a good chicken, rice and vegetables combo... he'd like to experiment in the kitchen, and the likes of me requesting plain meals would annoy him.

We'd a nice routine. Eat dinner... watch the Championship game that was live on TV... and then have Paul's rice pudding for dessert with coffee.

Those nights are some of my best memories in football, all hanging out and having a laugh. That group spirit translated to match day and I appreciated the importance of that atmosphere when I met with the exact opposite later at Reading. We always did stuff together at Hull... midweek cinema trips or meeting up after a Saturday game.

That core of players acted as our engine on the pitch but also monitored the dressing-room. The better relationship you have with players, the more honest you can be. There was no whispering around corners... we'd bawl each other out if needed. No one had hidden agendas. We were all there for the same thing.

It was a special group.

The first of my 191 games with Hull was away to Cardiff City on November 10, 2012. We lost 2-1 but the setback wasn't serious. Soon I was playing regularly. My knee felt good. With every match I played, I felt stronger and was in a great headspace. The confidence was sky high in the squad.

That December we won five times; I started every game and scored three times. My first goal as a senior pro in England arrived against Watford. Corry Evans took a shot that Manuel Almunia saved, sending the ball looping up into the air.

I saw the empty goal, jumped to head it... and the roar went up.

Scoring when your team wins is the biggest adrenaline rush. I repeated it against Huddersfield and Leeds, victories in local battles that sent the spirits of our fans soaring.

Bruce didn't want me to head back to Sunderland. Dad was happy I was playing the whole time. I felt it was a 50-50 call.

Hull was a special group but part of me relished the challenge to go back and fight for a place at Sunderland. Ultimately, the decision was made for me. Sunderland were looking to sign a Senegalese midfielder, Alfred N'Diaye, and were happy to sell me as part of their plans.

One in and one out, that's how transfer windows work.

Finalising the deal was complicated. After the loan period finished, I was told to go back to Sunderland first. Then my agent Neil Fewings called to say... 'Head to Hull'.

Another call... the fee couldn't be agreed... and I needed to return to Sunderland.

Up and down, driving on the A19 motorway.

Eventually it got done. I made the move on Tuesday, January 8, 2013, the same day as Robbie Brady permanently signed.

Neil was great in sorting everything. He looked after Jordan first and that opened the door for me to get him as my agent. When I signed for Hull, there was a stand-off as I'd a salary figure in my head. There was a difference of a thousand quid in the offer and Neil stuck in there for me to negotiate it. Every time I've really needed him, he's looked after me.

What I achieved with Hull, I'd love to have done with Sunderland, the club that had given me my break in England.

CHAPTER 6 • WELCOME TO HULL   83

But the decision was made. The loan move provided a taste of life with Hull and it felt good. Nothing changed when the move became permanent; the Hull players knew what they were getting and it was just about maintaining that form.

By May, we'd hit the target of top two in the table and I felt a strong part of that.

THE BEAUTY OF promotion is that the buzz lasts all summer long. When the fixture list came out, we started our season at the beginning of the second Jose Mourinho era. I played midfield against another Chelsea team loaded with talent... Frank Lampard, Kevin De Bruyne, Eden Hazard, Oscar and Fernando Torres.

Lampard missed a penalty, but then scored an outrageous free-kick. We lost 2-0 but had steadied after a rocky opening.

The 2013-14 season was a pivotal one.

After all the injury struggles and hardship, I became a Premier League regular... played 40 times for Hull, 30 of those in the league with 27 starts.

At 24 years old, I felt more established, but I had to rise to a challenge early that season. Signings are inevitable after you go up a division.

There was all this joy and elation after clinching promotion.

You get a pay rise and everything is great. When promotion is achieved, it can feel like the box is ticked. Fans and players are basking in the glow of celebration. For managers the question is how do we improve?

Can we bridge that gap to the Premier League?

You can work so hard to get somewhere, but the manager makes the decision to bring in top quality players to try help make us better. You go into the summer and, all of a sudden, the club is being linked with 10-15 different players.

I had played a lot of games in the Championship that previous season. I knew I had played such a huge part in us going up but there was a key question swirling around in my mind. *Is my place in the team safe?*

Clubs can get used to the Championship, the rhythms of the division and the particular styles of play. Then you come into the Premier League.

Look at any of the top 10 teams... they're all top quality sides. There's a reason why they have enjoyed that Premier League status for a long time. When a team gets promoted, all of a sudden you're on the backfoot, you're not going to be able to dominate possession or dictate the pace of the game.

Championship teams may have feared you but Premier League sides don't have that level of concern. Every Premier League side looks at the three teams promoted and eyes it as a straightforward task to get wins on the board. *We'll beat them home, we'll beat that side away… points in the bag.*

The question facing players coming up from the Championship is are they capable of adjusting to the bigger tests that lie ahead?

IN THE SUMMER of 2013, we signed two midfielders from Spurs, Jake Livermore and Tom Huddlestone. Two proven players who had been capped by England. I started that opening game against Chelsea and then I was out of the team for a few matches.

We often played three in the middle, so there was a spot up for grabs. That December our system clicked. Huddlestone sat deeper, I played more on the right and Jake was to the left. Jake's dad used to chat with my dad, he loved how we combined together.

We complemented each other, as myself and Jake did the running for Tom. He'd joke that he was the master in midfield holding two dogs… and he'd set us off at the start. We didn't like that analogy, but it was pretty accurate.

Jake had more in his locker, I was focused on my specific strengths… cover the pitch, win the ball and lay it off to Tom to spray.

I didn't need the headlines, I just needed to play and the team to succeed. It was the start of a strong midfield relationship.

Tom was probably the most naturally gifted player I ever played with. His ability was disgusting. Right foot, left foot, both passing and shooting, it was no effort to him. Could do it all.

He was at Hull between 2013 and '17… we soldiered together for a long time. Then he moved to Derby for a few years, went back to Hull and more recently joined Manchester United, as player-coach for their under-21s.

I only live up the road from the training ground, so during his second time as a Hull player, I used to see Tom all the time driving past in the morning to training. We always used to say we'd catch up and go for a round of golf, but it just didn't materialise. Life moves on for people. I'm based in Hull, he's from Nottingham, so that's his base where he would go home to.

We had a good midfield chemistry with Jake, and Stephen Quinn was an important member as well. People didn't realise how good Quinny was and he was a bargain for Hull at the low price he cost from Sheffield United. A great lad first and foremost, great to be around, always laughing and joking in the changing room. He was just another example of why that Hull squad gelled so well.

Our dressing-room remained strong, even though there were new personalities added to the mix after we'd been promoted. Curtis Davies and Allan McGregor also joined and slotted straight in. And Ahmed Elmohamady, who was on loan the season before, joined permanently.

Danny Graham joined on loan from Sunderland. He lived in my house for six months. I haven't seen him in years now… we both have kids and life moves on. But that period around 2013, we did everything together. Heading to training in the morning, heading home to hang out, have dinner every evening. He'd go up and down to Sunderland where his missus was still living, but I helped him out with a base in Hull. He was good company.

In January, Bruce targeted strikers and he brought in Shane Long and the Croatian Nikica Jelavić. They were important signings. Jelavić finished our top Premier League scorer with five goals… Shane got four. We needed help and they freshened us up.

Shane was a familiar figure from Ireland squads. He brought the Irish crew up to five… myself, Paul, Brady, Stephen Quinn and Longy. That dynamic was great, and we were all honest in our approach. Shane moved to Southampton the following August but he had fitted into the Hull mindset and worked hard.

Our group attitude kept us up that year.

The Fulham game was key at the end of April.

They were 19th and fighting for their lives, and we were down 2-0. Then Jelavić and Longy both scored in the last 15 minutes to secure the draw.

We lost our last three games, but we knew then we were okay and safe from relegation.

NOT EVERY SIGNING worked out. Hatem Ben Arfa moved on loan in September 2014. A five-time Ligue 1 winner, he had a big reputation.

His move was a disaster.

The day he signed, he turned up with his own camera crew, said he might make a documentary… wanted to record everything. We couldn't understand that attitude.

Hatem was so gifted that he wanted everyone to bow down to him. He was a phenomenal player, but he didn't care. Myself and Quinny got wound up one day, and had a full-blown argument with the coaches over the way Hatem trained. It started to filter back to Bruce that he was becoming a problem.

If he performed in games, we might have let it slide.

We played Man United at Old Trafford in November. He started and was subbed off after 35 minutes. He sat in the changing-room at half-time; Bruce was going mad and he just started laughing at him.

That was the end.

He went back to Newcastle and they eventually released him. He joined Nice and the following season in France scored 17 goals as they finished fourth to qualify for Europe. We saw none of that form.

I understand there is pressure on a player when they transfer into a club, particularly if there's a big fee involved. Asamoah Gyan was Sunderland's club record signing when he joined in August 2010 for a fee of £13million.

Asamoah was a really good lad. He got on really well with everyone. He spoke English, was very friendly, just had a way about him, all smiling and singing and dancing around the place. He never blew a training session off.

I wouldn't say Asamoah was a flop. He'd made such a name for himself at the World Cup with Ghana that summer in South Africa, scoring three goals as they reached the quarter-finals He didn't shoot the lights out in terms of getting goals for Sunderland, but still hit the net 10 times and he'd moments... like an equaliser against Newcastle in the 94th minute in January 2011 that was always going to draw praise. His effort levels were always good, people wouldn't turn on him in the dressing-room.

We got Gaston Ramirez on loan one season at Hull from Southampton. He was a Uruguayan midfielder, clearly a very good player. Good trainer, good lad, he got involved in the group dynamic. But we only saw glimpses of what he could do, Gaston just couldn't stay fit. He'd get himself into the starting team, he'd be doing well... and his hamstring would go. Out for six to eight weeks, then he'd get back fit again.

That was a disappointing one. I would love to have played more often with him but you need luck with injuries for that and my career has taught me not everyone gets those breaks.

In any walk of life, if you know someone is making an effort and trying their best and, you're in it together, then you'll appreciate that and respect that person. But when someone's tossing it off and they're looking for the same credit as you, that's not on.

You've got to pull your weight.

The best sport teams are full of star players that also put the work in. Look at Liverpool's brilliant front three of the last few years… Mo Salah, Sadio Mane and Roberto Firmino. They worked so hard out of possession.

Hatem was an incredible footballer, everyone could see that he when he joined Hull on loan. But he just didn't work hard enough. He'd view the whole thing as a laugh, dribbling around in training sessions and more focused on who he could nutmeg every day than anything else. I used to get so frustrated with him.

If I met him now, I'd still be disappointed that a player with so much ability didn't express that.

I loved my playing days with Hull City, and the likes of Harry Maguire and Andy Robertson (top) helped make us a team destined for the Premier League. Here we are celebrating promotion from the Championship (below).

GUIDING THE TIGERS BACK TO TOP FLIGHT

Euro 2016

MARTIN O'NEILL CLEARED his throat and prepared to speak. *It all comes down to this announcement.* Thirteen days out from Ireland's Euro 2016 opener against Sweden... and finally we will find out who's going to France.

Seems fitting in a way that I'm in a dressing-room at Turner's Cross!

The biggest moment in my international career and the news will be broken to me at my local stadium.

WE'VE JUST LOST 2-1 to Belarus, before a sell-out crowd in the sunshine for the last warm-up game. I haven't played well and now the fear of rejection is growing. I'm either packing my bags to head to Versailles, or I've got the summer off.

And if I do miss out, it's not like there's an instant chance to make amends. Major tournaments don't come around often for Ireland; a lot of our greatest players never went to a European Championships.

It's quiet in the room as the tension hangs in the air.

From the night we beat Bosnia in the play-off the previous November, I've been thinking about this moment. Anyone could have sat down then and written out the 17 or 18 bankers to make it.

Then you debate for the remaining seats on the plane.

Who's in and who's out?

If you're Seamus Coleman or Robbie Brady, you've just got to stay fit and be sharp when the summer comes around. For the rest of us, it's different. Four players for two midfield places… myself, Harry Arter, Stephen Quinn and Darron Gibson.

I don't want to be a hard luck story.

On the Saturday, Ireland had played Holland. Harry was excellent alongside Quinny. He hadn't played in the qualifiers but, suddenly, he's got a foot in the door and could make the squad.

At the same time, I was in Wembley celebrating Hull's promotion to the Premier League after the play-off final. Up until six in the morning, on the beer with my family, friends and teammates. Then, an early flight to Cork to meet with the Irish squad.

Martin played me against Belarus in midfield with Darron. I was all over the place; probably the worst game I've had in an Ireland shirt. Roy had a go at me after in private about my performance. *They needed more.*

It's justified… I was off the pace.

MARTIN HAS THE list in his hand.

'Right lads!' He rattles through the names.

You've got to concentrate. Sitting… head down… hands on knees. You're hanging on his every word, just waiting to hear your name called.

Then… 'David Meyler'.

That's it… I'm in.

It's a moment for celebration, but you must check yourself. There are lads who haven't made it. Myself and Quinn are selected. Harry, who has picked up an injury, and Darron miss out. It's hard on them.

The most heartbreaking omission is David Forde. He'd played in four qualifiers… the goalkeeper for the draw in Germany. Now he is out! That's how tough it is.

We're all grown men. You have to take it.

But it's dog-eat-dog.

It's me or you. *I'm going to make sure it's me.*

That's professional sport. People don't want to admit it, but it's a very cruel business.

I leave after and meet dad outside.

ANOTHER SQUAD ANNOUNCEMENT many years before comes to mind. In 2002, I got asked to captain the Cork Kennedy Cup team in Limerick.

A huge deal for a 13-year-old.

Then, the 20-player squad was read out for the tournament… 'David Meyler' is not called out.

The lads who hadn't made the cut were politely asked to leave. I headed over to the car and told dad I wasn't in the squad, despite the captaincy invite.

Turned out it was just a big mistake. The coach read the list wrong.

I got called back, but that five-minute wait wasn't enjoyable.

Now the stakes are higher.

'Are you going?' asks dad.

'Yeah.'

'Well, thank God for that!' By his reaction, I can tell he wasn't confident either.

AFTER THE DRAW with Germany in 2014, we headed to Glasgow in November with a bounce in our step. Celtic Park was a ground I loved and had sampled the atmosphere on Celtic's big European nights.

I was desperate to play but spent the game on the bench. Quinny and Robbie were brought on in midfield.

The worst thing was we lost 1-0.

Martin went bananas over the goal we conceded; I lost count of the amount of meetings we had afterwards about that game.

There was an edge to the mood in the crowd that night… felt like it could kick off at any stage. It only needed one moment to light the fuse, and Scotland provided it with their goal. Shaun Maloney took a short corner, played a one-two with Scott Brown… before curling a shot into the far corner in the 75th minute.

It was a lovely finish but Aiden McGeady came off the back post. If he stays there, he blocks the shot. Martin was raging… not doing the basics at set-pieces had cost us.

The result was a proper kick in the teeth.

The year ended on a nice note.

Four days later, Martin called me in at the team hotel in Dublin. He was making me captain for the friendly against the USA. He told me it was because of the job I'd done for him in Germany.

The personal honour was huge but my reaction was low-key. That was deliberate. I only told dad. It all goes back to the Ireland under-21s when we played Turkey once in Cork, and I got taken off at half-time after one of the worst games of my career.

Before the game I must have sorted 60 people with tickets. Even that morning and lunchtime, I was racing around, thinking… *This is great…*

I'm in Cork, I'm playing for Ireland… who wants tickets?

Just let me know, I'll sort you.

Everyone came to watch me play and I was hauled off before the second-half started. Dad hit the roof after. Ever since, I just sort him, mum and Sarah.

Let them look after everyone else.

SO, CAPTAINING IRELAND wasn't my focus… performing in the game was. It went brilliantly. We won 4-1. Robbie Brady scored a cracker of a free-kick to round it off.

And after, I could reflect on the captaincy role, the trust Martin placed in me when he could very easily have made someone like Shay Given captain that night. It's difficult to describe the emotion of it and that feeling swelled further when I got to captain Ireland in the qualifiers a few years after.

Mary O'Brien, who worked with the FAI, got me the pennant from the USA game. I'm not sure was she meant to, but Mary appreciated the small details. A lovely touch… it's at home now in Cork in a frame with the armband and the jersey from that night.

SIMPLE INSTRUCTIONS. STEPHEN Ward is coming off injured.

Go in and shore up that midfield.

Keep it steady, stay with the runners. I'm nodding and listening to Martin on the sideline.

October 2015.

0-0 against Germany… 69 minutes. And I'm in.

Seconds later, Germany win the ball in their box and try to counter-attack. Marco Reus makes a run… John O'Shea gets a foot in and the ball rolls loose to me. Quick thought… *Am I getting pressed?*

Think I'll send it back to Darren Randolph.

I turn as Randolph boots it and watch on. Shane Long is lightning quick. The ball hits his left shin and falls perfectly as he's gone past the German defence.

He blasts it past Manuel Neuer… 70 minutes and it's 1-0. There's a split second pause and a huge roar erupts. He's scored!

We're beating Germany! This is unbelievable!

And then I wonder how we're going to hold on? Drawing or losing to Germany in the last 20 minutes is different to this. Now we've got something to protect and that creates a greater fear. *Don't be the one that makes a mistake.*

That same thought is on everyone's mind. We're under siege and everyone's shouting.

'COME IN!'

'PUSH!'

'PRESS!'

'DROP!'

Goalkeeper, back four and midfield all need to be in line and switched on. Germany have enough talent without us making it easy for them.

Seventy-seven minutes.

Toni Kroos and Mesut Özil work it on the wing. I'm keeping an eye to my left on Thomas Müller. Then Jonas Hector gets to the byline and drags it back.

Reus and O'Shea go for it but they both miss the ball. I'm caught by surprise… stick out my left leg and it rolls past me towards Müller.

I fall and can only sit in the box watching him.

A second frozen in time. Müller has the chance to pick his spot; this outstanding player who has scored 30 goals for Germany and 10 in the World Cup. He side-foots it and I turn to watch the ball fly past the post; relief rushing through my body as I realise… *He's missed.*

Got away with it.

But I can hear Martin and Roy roaring at me.

I'm hungry and alert for the rest of the game. This is my chance after those games sitting on the bench in Glasgow and Faro and Dublin. *We must not concede.*

Germany have all the possession but there's no way through… the final whistle blasts. We have beaten the world champions and secured a play-off for the Euros.

Later, at the team hotel in Malahide, we have a few pints and try to make sense of it. My phone is going off the wall. From family to some fella in the middle of nowhere in Australia that you went to school with, everyone is messaging… everyone has watched the game and everyone is celebrating the win.

Fairytale stuff.

REGRETS? THEY DON'T haunt me from Euro 2016, but they are there.

I didn't get any game time. Only four of the squad didn't play and two were goalkeepers – myself, Cyrus Christie, Shay and Kieren Westwood. There was an opportunity after the Belgium game to force my way in. I didn't do enough.

It's easier said than done with the games coming thick and fast, but I should have done more in training.

We were at the team base in Versailles after a session one day and I headed back to my room. A few hours downtime… I sat there with the PlayStation, headset on, talking to my friends.

All the players stayed on the one floor and the doors were left on the latch. I heard a rumble at the door and called out… 'IT'S OPEN'

I turn and, next thing, I just see Roy standing there.

Jump up. Whip off the headset.

Drop the controller.

Roy is frustrated with the way I'd trained. We were preparing to play Belgium and he wanted to see more… for me to push myself.

He was right. Roy was reminding me not to get comfortable. I had almost slipped into the mindset of an Irish fan away at the Euros, just there to enjoy the ride. That may sound harsh, but it is the truth.

Hindsight is a beautiful thing. I had put so much into making the squad, that getting to France felt like an achievement. Working to get my hamstring right in April, pushing for the play-offs and that Irish squad spot in May.

I realised those goals, but in June I forgot to set another target.

When the tournament started, I was just glad to be in that 23-man bubble. Being involved is something I'll always look back on with great pride but if we'd reached the 2018 World Cup, my mindset would have been completely different. At the Euros I was happy to be there and before I knew it… it was all over.

The moments were still special, and I loved being an eyewitness.

Wes striking the ball sweetly in Paris against Sweden after Seamus had clipped the ball across. Taking on France in Lyon and going in front. Bordeaux was awful. Belgium hammering us out the gate, but that meant Lille ended up being a night of total euphoria.

Sitting on the bench at the Stade Pierre-Mauroy, when Wes misses the chance and thinking… *That's it. Pack up and go home.*

Then he picks up the ball, puts it on a sixpence and Robbie heads it in.

Absolute magic.

I ran so far onto the pitch in celebration after the goal, I should nearly have got a cap.

We were always capable of digging out a result when it mattered. A goal for Ireland like that lifts the country to a state of sporting happiness that rarely comes around. The mood in the dressing-room after was electric. For a tournament everyone has their friends and family there, that adds to the emotion.

We had all grown up on tales of Euro 88 and Italia 90. Now we were all together, experiencing an Irish international football night that would not be forgotten.

OFTEN, INJURED IRELAND players will not go to home games.

It's a personal choice. They'll stay in England with their clubs and get treatment. I preferred to be there, let the Ireland management know that I wanted to be with the squad. A throwback to my Sunderland days after damaging my cruciate.

It helped mentally to be there, as tough as it was not being available.

In November 2015, in the week building up to our Euro play-off against Bosnia, I collided with Marc Wilson in training. Innocuous enough but I paid a price… Grade 2 tear of the medial ligament in my right knee and I was out for the two legs.

I watched the first game on the Friday night in the East Village Bar at home in Douglas, as the lads drew 1-1 in the fog in Zenica, with Robbie scoring. Then, straight to Dublin before the second-leg on the Monday night.

I used to always find myself in the snack room of the team hotel the night before games. Bowl of cereal, slice of toast or cup of tea before bed.

Martin would often be there and we'd get chatting. For that Bosnia second-leg I wasn't playing and so, in no rush to get some sleep, we sat and talked for the bones of an hour.

I always had great conversations with Martin about football. Those were the best times. There was a perception that Martin constantly harked back to his playing days. He did it occasionally. You can only reflect on your own football journey.

Martin was a two-time European Cup winner, played in the 1982 World Cup when Northern Ireland beat Spain. If you can't draw on those experiences, what can you draw on?

I liked picking his brain to hear about his football experiences. Stories about Nottingham Forest's incredible runs that saw them win the finals of the old European Cup in 1979 and '80. The great Liverpool team he had played against, filled with so many brilliant players. The type of midfield play in those times, the qualities that were required to succeed.

As a boy, I was a huge Celtic fan and Martin managed that team I idolized… Henrik Larsson, Neil Lennon and Stiliyan Petrov. I signed up to The Huddle Group, a supporters' club.

Birthday and Christmas cards would come through the letterbox in Cork with Martin's signature on them. He'd laugh when I brought that up and recall the Celtic secretary giving him a pile of cards to scribble his name on.

He had fascinating stories about the Leicester City side in the 90s, and the Aston Villa team later. People forget footballers start out as fans.

I loved listening to all that.

He was nervous about the Bosnia game, mindful of their star names… Eden Džeko and Miralem Pjanić. I felt the lads looked good and sharp; told him not to worry, we were going to win. I even predicted the right scoreline… 2-0.

After the match ended and Jon Walters had scored the key goals, I hobbled down to the side of the pitch on crutches, my right knee in a brace. Martin was hugging all his staff. He spotted me… I hug him and he says, 'You were right!'

On the pitch for the lap of honour and in the dressing-room after, is as happy as I have felt in football. We had done it.

Qualified for a major international tournament.

If you could only bottle the feeling of that night in Dublin to relive it all over again.

The family flag on tour at Euro 2016, and Martin O'Neill presents me with some of my Ireland caps.

Captaining Ireland was the greatest thrill of my football career and here I am (above) with Martin O'Neill before the World Cup qualifier second-leg against Denmark in the Aviva Stadium; and (right) in action in the game.

DAD'S SEAT

DAD GENERALLY SAT in the lower West Stand.

He had his two main spots, not far behind either dugout, close to the tunnel where the players came out. Spent a couple of seasons mainly sitting near the away dugout and a couple closer to the home dugout. It was in the section where all the families of the players sat... the club would designate an area in the stand for them to sit for the home games and sort out the tickets then.

I'd always be able to pick him out in the crowd.

You couldn't miss him. Dad would be present for the warm-ups, he would study them... keeping an eye on how players were moving. A lot of fans wouldn't be in for that, they're late arrivals. Dad would be in his seat by then.

I'd have left his ticket at the club office to collect for those games. He'd be waiting when the team bus would arrive for away games and I'd hand him the ticket.

Dad was always there, just a constant presence.

He liked the matchday experience. Before or after the game he might go into the players' lounge for a quick bite to eat and cup of tea. He'd get to meet a lot of the other players' families in there.

I always went into the players' lounge after because you've still got anywhere between 18,000 and 22,000 people leaving the stadium. By the time we got in after the final whistle, we'd have a debrief with the manager, get showered, get changed... then I'd head into the lounge.

A lot of the time dad was leaving soon after to get back to make his flight home. The only time I might get to see him and chat were the 15 or 20 minutes in the players' lounge after. Then he'd be off... jump in the car and head back home.

I always enjoyed seeing him. I look back on that time we had together fondly. We'd often speak about it later that he felt he should have stayed more, spent the night and got the first flight home in the morning. At the time I get that he didn't want to bother me and be imposing.

I do appreciate the sacrifices he made for me. We might have different things going on but the times he did stay were great... we could have had a good result and head out for dinner after. He'd a lot going on himself with all the teams he was coaching and managing back in Ireland; his time was precious.

Sometimes, he might leave in the 75th minute of a match to beat the traffic to get back to the airport in time for his flight. To think he went to all that trouble to come to see a game seems ludicrous.

But everyone used to say to me it was unbelievable. All the other players, management and staff connected with the club would notice dad was constantly at the games. Robert Snodgrass used to say his parents had been to only a couple of games in his career. For different reasons they couldn't go... they were from Glasgow, he was playing for clubs like Leeds and Hull, it wasn't exactly a short, straightforward trip. His brothers and sisters would regularly come to his games, the parents would mind their kids those times. Snodgrass used to always tell me it was amazing that my dad was over to so many games.

PEOPLE WOULD OFTEN comment to dad that there was a danger he was putting too much pressure on me by being that presence every weekend in the stadium. I never felt any added pressure, though. I was so used to him being there, it was more strange when he wasn't present. In those situations, he would be so apologetic for not being able to make it.

In 2016, he couldn't make the play-off final at Wembley because one of the hurling teams he was managing had an important match the same day in Ireland.

I was never weighed down by the thought that dad has made the trip over and I must give a performance to justify that effort. I think I only let him down once. That was September 2015... we lost 1-0 away to Brighton in the Championship.

He'd flown over to London, headed to the south coast to watch the game and I was taken off after half hour. Dad didn't really speak to me after. The manager lambasted me at half-time for how I'd played, then after watching the game back he apologised to me on the Monday as it hadn't really been my fault.

When I'd played well and Hull had won the match, that was the beauty of my experience as a footballer to be able to walk into the players' lounge after... and see dad there. I often think it is a shame from having retired early that I can't still be playing now for a club and get to head in after the match with my kids there to see me.

On the odd occasion I'd have gone into the players' lounge before the game to see how he was, checking if everything had been alright with the trip. If Cally was coming to the match I'd tell him and she'd usually join around 2pm then. My mum would come with dad sometimes. She was at the game around Christmas 2013 when I scored against Manchester United. She had this habit, where she came to four games and I scored in them all. At the end of that run dad was saying she was coming every week.

Dermot Lynch, a friend of my dad's, flew over with him once for an FA Cup game... fifth round against Arsenal. It was a replay, away at the Emirates we'd drawn 0-0. Then we got battered 4-0 at home. Dad was joking after that Dermot was a bad omen, said he wasn't coming again.

THE HULL GAMES were significant for dad, but I think the Ireland games stood out for mum and my sister Sarah. Mum was in Gelsenkirchen when we drew with Germany; the emotion of that was amazing. Then for Sarah it was the Wales game in Cardiff where all the family were together.

All the stars aligned that night.

It wasn't often all the family were able to get together to watch me. They were all there in London for the FA Cup final with the group of buddies from home who wore Hull jerseys with 'Meyler 7' on the back. They'd come up with the idea of getting the jerseys for the day, but then asked me to sort them out... and so I ended up trying to get Hull City kit in all different sizes for them that week.

It's a great memory though having them all over... the night ending back at the hotel with all the lads there singing away with Steve Bruce and Niall Quinn.

Kelogs nudging everyone on... 'Go on Quinny, sing us a song there'.

Kelogs would be great for a sing-song, he wouldn't have a note in his head but he'd be getting everyone else going.

The day we got promoted in 2013 and we had to wait for the result from the Watford game, the only person I wanted to be with was dad. He'd been at every game and was in his usual spot in the West Stand. Someone who'd been so important in my journey.

When news came through that the result had gone our way and the whole stadium erupted in joy, myself, dad and Kelogs just fell into this hug. A really beautiful moment. That was the greatest day here as a footballer. There was so much emotion because of what was at stake. The tension beforehand, the nervousness during it... the hope when we scored goals, the despair when they equalised... the torture of having to wait for the other scoreline, and then the crazy celebrations afterwards.

When you achieve your goal in football, whatever it may be, and in our case it was promotion to the Premier League, everyone involved is on cloud nine. It's a feeling that lives with you... bonds you with that playing group, the management, the fans and everyone connected to the club forever.

People still come up to me on the street about it.

Pride and Passion

MY CAREER REVOLVED around two clubs.

Sunderland in Durham right up in the north-east of England… Hull a couple of hours south of there in East Yorkshire. I identified with those places in the north. Maybe that's my upbringing in Cork… the second city in Ireland, that's where my home was.

A lot of players want to gravitate to the capital in the south.

London was not a place for me on a long-term basis. Too busy. Too frantic. Too much going on. Settling and playing for a club there was not something I was pushing for.

I like to be there for a short time, dip my toe in and get out.

Every now and again, we'll head down there as a family, catch a show, get a bite to eat, show the kids around. It's great… love it. But, I know there's an expiration date to the trip. Head down on a Friday… I'm coming back home on a Sunday.

WHEN I PLAYED for Reading in that brief spell, I didn't base myself in Central London. I lived out near Ascot.

That was fine, but the pace of life was still up a few notches.

There's definitely a different vibe to southern and northern people in England. I find the people around the Hull area a lot more friendly. Life moves at a slower, nicer pace up here. It's peaceful.

I used to find it fascinating when I went down to work in London for Uncut or Sky Sports… getting off the train at King's Cross, just a world of chaos. Everyone is racing around, on the move, heading somewhere else.

Some people love that sense of urgency and fast-paced life. I'm just in the opposite camp. I like city life for short periods, and I love trips to New York for instance. But as a base, I need something different.

Hull offers me that.

SUNDERLAND WAS THE same.

The only difference to the atmosphere there was the football and the elevated status it enjoys. The people work Monday to Friday, go to a game on a Saturday, spend time with family on a Sunday… and then repeat the cycle all over again the next week.

Football is their world.

The Netflix series *Sunderland 'til I Die* opens a window into that. A very good friend of mine is Johnny Small… his father Duncan is a taxi driver up there, Station Taxis. He's an example of someone who lives and breathes Sunderland FC.

Look at the crowds they brought for the play-offs last May, the crowd that followed them down to Wembley when they beat Wycombe 2-0 and clinched promotion. It's phenomenal.

It is life and death for them.

The Sunderland-Newcastle rivalry is intense. North-East neighbours. I actually have great admiration for both sets of fans, but obviously my affiliation is to Sunderland because I lived there and played for them, and they were very good to me.

In October 2010, we lost 5-1 away to Newcastle.

I was out injured at the time trying to get my cruciate right. The game was a nightmare for the club. We were down 3-0 at half-time. Titus Bramble got sent-off early in the second-half. Newcastle scored another two goals… Kevin Nolan completing a hat-trick.

By the time Darren Bent scored in the 90th minute, it was just a consolation. I can still see the couple of thousand Sunderland fans rushing down to throw their season tickets at the dugout towards Steve Bruce, a river of abuse and criticism flowing down from the stand.

The Tyne-Wear derby game defines the season if Sunderland and Newcastle come across each other. Middlesbrough is about 40 minutes south, but 15 miles separate the Stadium of Light and St James' Park, so I understood that Newcastle was the local fixture that carried greater meaning.

I've often tried to compare it to other sporting rivalries that I experienced. Back home in Ireland, the gaelic football teams of Cork and Kerry had a huge rivalry when I was young, both playing each other in the finals of the Munster Championship.

I witnessed that as I grew up, but with the Sunderland-Newcastle relationship, that rivalry felt greater. There was more energy to it, more passion and more significance for those involved.

I was close enough to understand the Sunderland-Newcastle rivalry but never experienced it first-hand. We played Newcastle seven times during my time at Sunderland. The first few occasions I was only recently joined from Cork City and not in the first team picture. Then the cruciate injury wrecked my plans for a long time. In March 2012 and October 2012, I was on the bench home and away for two derbies, both games ending in 1-1 draws. I wasn't brought on in either game.

I did play for Sunderland in a reserve game against Newcastle... midfield in November 2011 at the Stadium of Light. Even for a level below the top, you could see it meant something to the fans that were there. I had Irish teammates playing in John Egan and James McClean... Ryan Noble scored a hat-trick in our 3-0 win.

Looking back, it was still nice to get a sense of what the occasion was about. The Sunderland bus pulling into St James' Park, fans screaming and throwing stuff at the windows. Or I'd look out my apartment window in Sunderland and see a few thousand Newcastle fans arriving into the city from the train station and being ushered by lines of police up to the stadium.

What an atmosphere.

I loved that. Give me fans roaring before kick-off, whipping the whole place up into a frenzy. There's a few examples of that in football... I've been at Anfield on those special midweek European nights when the whole place is on edge with anticipation before it starts. The Tyne-Wear derby felt like that.

I went to a couple games in St James' Park, in the away end with Sunderland fans, up in the sky looking down at the pitch. They won them both 3-0... April 2013 with Paolo Di Canio in charge, February 2014 when Gus Poyet was manager.

I WAS A Hull player then, but still had a connection with Sunderland, and remained really good friends with Johnny Small, who I got to know through Jordan. The beautiful thing was, those derbies were always on at noon on a Sunday. I'd play for Hull on Saturday afternoon, drive up Saturday night and go out with Johnny... then we'd go to the game on Sunday.

We'd slip in amongst the few thousand Sunderland fans.

I got recognised but never hassled. I was playing for a club in another division, so no issue being amongst them and with Sunderland winning, that's all they cared about. I always made sure to look neutral, never wore any club colours and told the lads with me to do the same. Then afterwards, as the police tried to escort the away fans together, we could divert off, get into the car and leave unnoticed.

There was an edge to the post-match mood after those games. One of them was the infamous incident when a Newcastle fan punched a police horse, which happened just up the road from where we were at the time.

Retaining that link to the fan matchday experience was important to me. When I retired, I said to Cally one of my sporting bucket list items was to go to an away Champions League game as a Liverpool fan... I was desperate to do that. Go to a game, few drinks beforehand, soak up the anticipation... get lost in the atmosphere, not worrying about your image or as a player having to mentally prepare for it. Just go and watch a game.

I went to see Liverpool play against Atletico Madrid in the Metropolitano in February 2020, and had been at the same stadium the previous June for the Champions League final against Tottenham. Going around the fan-zones before that final in Madrid was amazing. The buzz before that game was incredible and it was great to be witnessing a match build-up on the other side.

I say this to people in the North-East all the time and they'll often dismiss it, but Sunderland need Newcastle and Newcastle need Sunderland.

Of course the dynamic has changed. The world is Newcastle's oyster now because of the financial firepower they have. You get the thousands of Geordie fans behind them, add in the quality of players and you'd wonder how far they will go.

The financial backing Newcastle have received has sparked debate, just like it does for every club in this situation. I don't think it's something players care too much or concern themselves about as to where the money is coming from. They're there to do a job and pick up their salary.

Should the players in that situation have to answer questions about the source of the money that is being pumped into their club? There's a case for yes and a case for no. These are decisions made above them.

If I was playing for Newcastle, I would stress that picking the owners has nothing to do with me. It's down to the FA to examine where the money going into football clubs goes to and judge whether to object or not. Do I think the way some things are in Saudi Arabia is right or wrong? Of course I think they're wrong, but I would question what impact one individual can make.

The concept of loyalty in football has become less, players are only responsible for themselves. The World Cup in Qatar has generated a lot of criticism. I completely understand the questions being raised and the issues that are justifiably talked about. I still feel as an ex-Ireland player, if we had qualified, everyone would have focused on the team, fans would have travelled over, and the performances of the team would have been the main talking point.

As a player, there are so many different dimensions now to football, between business and political decisions, and a player has absolutely no control over any of this.

Football is their job.

They are there to do *that* job.

Playing with Sunderland and Hull allowed me to appreciate the true nature of passionate football fans in England. Scoring was important, but always putting a shift in was something I fully understood.

A FOOTBALL LIFE

A FEW YEARS back, I had some time off and made a quick trip home to Cork. One of the nights I ended up out on the beer with the lads. We'd a good time and enjoyed ourselves.

When you leave Havana Browns nightclub in the city centre, you come out to an alley.

I was full to the brim that night as I headed out the door, and went in search of food. There was a Subway open. Perfect.

Got my food, then sat down on the path on the side of the road to eat it. Normal enough late-night scene of a lad swaying side to side, but causing no one any harm.

A few young lads came over hassling me. I just tried to get rid of them, but someone took out their phone and recorded a video.

The problem was they put it somewhere the whole world could see. It was viewed over 100,000 times on Facebook. Nothing out of the ordinary... the footage just showed 'David' after he'd had a few too many.

But football meant I had a name and reputation and, before all that, I had a family. My parents saw it... my mother got upset. The kid thought he was having a laugh throwing that video up on the internet and didn't realise the repercussions.

He got in touch after to apologise and took the video down.

The damage was done though. It was too late.

FOOTBALL HAS OPENED doors for me to meet people I admired that I wouldn't otherwise come into contact with.

Jordan is a very private person, not too close with too many footballers. Steven Gerrard knew I was good mates with him, so put two and two together. I got accepted by association and we'd chat if I was at Liverpool's training ground with Jordan. It pained me as a Celtic fan to see him with Rangers but I wanted to see him do well. I'd speak to him every now and again.

He invited me over to play in a golf day he runs in Portugal at the Laranjal Course in Quinta do Lago. You get opportunities like that due to a level of fame, but I knew I wasn't a household name and at times got reminded of it.

Kelogs came with me for that trip; we got collected at the airport and brought to the complex of nice apartments where we were staying. We were eager to get a feel for the course, so went to play a few holes the day before and met a few people. Max Rushden was there... he's a talkSPORT presenter and hosts *The Football Weekly* podcast. He introduced himself.

'Hi I'm Max. What's your name?'

'I'm David.'

'Oh, so what do you do?'

'I play football.'

'I should probably know that yeah. Who do you play for?'

'Hull and Ireland.'

'Yeah... clearly I'm not very good at my job!'

We started laughing about it. I heard him later joke I wasn't in kit and it was pre the Pardew headbutt, an incident which did make me known. Max hasn't forgotten me since anyway, so that's a good thing.

AS I GREW older, I felt I needed to be more careful in public. I was fully aware that I was in a position of privilege with the job and lifestyle I had, but at times found it difficult when people didn't respect privacy and often felt they were entitled to something.

There are flashpoints, mainly when you're out at night and drink is added to the equation. Fellas sticking phones in your face trying to take photos.

When I'm home, I want to just catch up with my friends since school. Talking non-stop to strangers about the form of Man United or Liverpool is not high on my agenda. Fellas might have a pop off me if I didn't engage in full-blown conversation at 1am.

To them, you're rude and ignorant, but I wonder how often they walk up to random people they don't know in other situations and expect them to talk.

I always felt it reasonable to prioritise my friends on a night out.

The money that a Premier League footballer earns will naturally make you a target. A fella approached me one night in a bar in Cork.

'You're a f****ng asshole the way you go on, coming home here and buying loads of drinks.'

I painted a picture for him... 'Only see these lads a few times a year... fortunate to have a good salary. Why not share that... take them all out for a night?

'Wouldn't you do the same for your friends... if you could?' He understood.

'Ah yeah. I'm sorry Dave. You're actually alright, like.'

It didn't always work out as peacefully as that. Havana Browns was our usual spot. Paul Montgomery owned it; then you had the lads... Skinner, Sully and James Dullea running it. The boys were great in looking after us.

My mates used to save me in their phones as 'queue jumper'.

We were well looked after and I met so many great people over the years. Back in your hometown and people genuinely wishing you well, congratulating you on a latest win, just treating me with respect. I really appreciated that.

But, unfortunately, the other side stays with you more.

So, you learn to take yourself out of those situations. I got more mature and started going out less. If I was heading out in Cork, we had a clear plan in place for the night. The Havanas staff would be sound in letting us stay behind for 15 minutes after they closed up, so we weren't coming out early on a Sunday morning when Cork city is pouring onto the streets from the bars and clubs.

Then we'd run out, jump straight into a taxi and go home. I got older and wiser and stayed out of trouble.

I WAS FORTUNATE I settled and integrated so well into the areas when I played football. For others, it was more difficult. At the 2010 World Cup, Paraguay had an excellent tournament, losing a quarter-final to eventual winners Spain.

Paulo da Silva already played for us, a defender who'd joined in 2009, and then the club signed another Paraguayan after that tournament in midfielder Cristian Riveros. He had been sensational that summer in South Africa but joining us was a nightmare for him. The style of football, the north-east weather and the language barrier all affected him.

You head into training, it's freezing cold, you don't understand what lads are saying in the changing room... and you can't get your football going on the pitch.

It was a real struggle.

I wondered at the time, how hard would I have found it if I had to move to Russia or somewhere? The move to England is a challenge but more comfortable for Irish lads like me. It was no surprise in January 2011 when Paulo went to Spain, and then Cristian moved to Turkey in June.

It's an issue with a lot of foreign players coming to England... they want the big city move, and their families can drive that, so life will be easier off the pitch. London, Manchester, Liverpool... these places are all attractive.

I played up north in Sunderland and Hull. London is a diverse place, but in Sunderland you've got mad Mackems everywhere. You have to immerse yourself in that atmosphere. I even saw some English players from down south struggling when they moved up.

You will help dictate the mood of a community. Walk down a street in London and you can step outside your life as a footballer, but not up here.

I had a good bond with Sunderland fans, but got a huge break in October 2011. The relationship could easily have been soured in a big way.

That summer I was in recovery mode from my second cruciate. My comeback was on the first of October, a last-minute sub in a 2-2 draw with West Brom. I sat out the next few games and then the month ended at home to Aston Villa.

I trained on the Friday as usual and was told to be in Saturday morning for a light session. Frazier Campbell was in the same boat, as we were doing rehab on our knees together. He suggested we should mark the end of the week, head to Jesmond in Newcastle and have a few drinks. Great shout.

We'd do recovery in the morning, grab lunch and watch the match.

The plan was to head home about 6pm that Friday. By 11pm we were both still out and well on our way. Eventually, we jumped in a taxi and I crashed in Frazier's house. We'd often do that, make sure we were together if we were going to be late for training the next morning.

We woke up on the Saturday and felt rough but got through the training work, had food and rocked down to the stadium. We went to the match day sponsors event, the usual meet and greet with people.

Then Nadia, who was running the event for the club, came up to me.

'David, you're wanted downstairs by the manager.'

My mind was racing as I went down

'Get your gear on... you're involved today!'

I sat in the changing room with all these fears running through my head. My preparation consisted of a day on the beer, a training session that morning and a full dinner an hour before. I was in no fit state to play.

Phil Bardsley was next to me and clocked straight away I'd been out. Soon other players did too.

The saving grace was being on the bench... surely just there to make up the numbers? Never coming on. But in the second-half, the shout came to warm up and in the 81st minute, I'm brought on.

Running onto the pitch, I was petrified how it was going to go. Shay Given took a goal-kick for Villa. Our back four were playing high but then retreated and roared at the midfield.

'DROP... DROP!'

I heard the instructions, jogged back... and tripped over my own feet... left sprawled on the pitch.

Richard Dunne put Villa 2-1 up a few minutes later but Stéphane Sességnon saved the day with an 89th minute header for the draw. I'd survived.

There was just one problem. On the Friday night I'd met a Sunderland season ticket holder in the pub; a lovely fella and we chatted away. Obviously, he's at the game on the Saturday and sees me playing near the end.

He got in touch with the club to complain about me being on the drink.

Perfectly fair.

Monday morning, I report for training and get summoned straight to Steve Bruce's office. A long walk upstairs.

Could be game over here, Dave.

You'll do well to explain your way out of this one.

The beauty of Steve Bruce's management was that he could draw on his playing experiences. He told me a story about playing for Man United, when he was out for a few games as he was due an operation. He went wine-tasting with his wife one day and ended up having a lash of pints after. Turned up at the match and there was a defender ruled out late on, so Bruce was thrown in to start.

'But don't you ever go drinking the night before a game again... even if you are injured!'

It was just a freak incident. I had genuinely been told I wouldn't be in the first- team, then I got dragged in last minute and end up playing a Premier League match hungover. No one ripped into me, they appreciated the confusion.

But it was only okay because I hadn't made some mistake that cost the team a goal and a result.

I was a lucky lad.

Make or Break

I DIDN'T WANT the Blackburn game in December 2009 to be a one-off with Sunderland. A debut appearance and then not heard of again. Fellas were coming back from injury and suspension. I had to stay involved. I played in an FA Cup win against Barrow in early January but wanted more big-time experiences. In the space of a month, I got them, and received some harsh lessons.

First up was a return to Stamford Bridge.

Unlike November 2008, this time I started against Chelsea. The changing room was small, so Bruce called me and Jordan into the shower area for a chat beforehand.

'Right Meyler, you're up against Frank Lampard!

'Jordan you're on Michael Ballack!

'Two wonderful players… but I think we've seen the best of their careers… ye'll be fine.' Then, after half an hour, Lampard is celebrating after scoring.

We were 4-0 down.

He finished with two goals… Ballack got one. We ended up losing 7-2.

It was an eye-opener to witness these fellas up close. The way they kept the ball in midfield was mesmerizing. It would have been easy for Bruce to whip us off but he left us on to learn. I know we got destroyed, but it was a brilliant learning experience.

After the game, myself and Jordan both met dad. I'm sure it wasn't the greatest game for him to sit through, watching players run rings around his son in the middle of the pitch. He was upbeat though.

'Lads, ye'll learn from it.

'Ye were playing two of the best. But why didn't ye get after them… properly get stuck in?'

My reply was simple.

'I couldn't even see the ball dad, at times… it was going that fast around me!'

YOU HAVE TO dust yourself down after a game like that. They were one of the best teams to ever play in the Premier League. Under Carlo Ancelotti, they were top of the table and won the league that year.

If people were understanding then, soon it was in short supply. In February in Fratton Park, I came on against Portsmouth. They were bottom of the table and the stakes were high. The game started positively for us. They had Ricardo Rocha sent-off. Benty scored a penalty to put us ahead.

So far, so good. We went down to 10 men early in the second-half, when Lee Cattermole got a second yellow card.

Eighty-five minutes in, and I was sent on for Andy Reid. I went in left side of midfield to shore things up… *and let's head home with the three points.*

I only lasted 115 seconds.

Craig Gordon hoofed a kickout towards the left wing. Steve Finnan was full-back for Portsmouth; it looked like he was going to head it but then he momentarily dropped back. I miscalculated, jumped in, leading with my forearm and caught him on the face.

Finnan got ratty, but there was no intention.

I had just mistimed it… a young fella in off the bench and eager to get into the game. I turned around and the referee Kevin Friend showed me a red card.

Eighty-seventh minute, and it was 9 versus 10, with plenty of injury-time. We were hanging on. Then Aruna Dindane headed in a Portsmouth equaliser in the 95th minute… 1-1, the place went wild. A full-blown disaster for me.

By that stage, I had gone off down the tunnel and Cattermole was in the changing room when I walked in.

'Oh, are we finished… did we win?'

'No, I've been sent-off.'

'YOU WHAT?!'

At that age, I had no clue of the pressure a manager might be under. That would have been a valuable three points. We finished the season 13th, clear of relegation but that was the sort of game which could have eased concerns.

Bruce came in after. It was the first time I took a proper bollocking off him.

He ripped me apart, but I had to take it. There was worse to follow.

Dad was at the game and we met after.

'I hope you're ready for the shit-show that's going to come now!'

That's when I understood how obsessive Sunderland fans were. The view was I'd cost the team the win. The abuse I received was outrageous. Going to the bus after the game… days later on the street… messages on Facebook and Twitter.

Horrible stuff.

It was a wake-up call to see their passion spill over into absolute vitriol. I could have gone two ways but took it in my stride and vowed I'd prove that I cared for the club.

I ONLY GOT sent-off twice more in my career. Straight red against Swansea in April 2015… a double booking against Norwich in October 2017.

The Portsmouth sending-off was deserved; for the other two I was unlucky. When I tackled Swansea's Kyle Naughton, my foot hit the top of the ball, popped off, came down and I shattered his ankle.

I felt bad about it; his ankle wasn't in a good way. After I'd been sent-off I went into the shower to get changed. He had to get his ankle treated. There was a TV in the corridor. I ended up sitting next to him watching the rest of the game. I felt awful… his ankle was swollen and he needed crutches.

I was apologising and he was saying not to worry, joking he should be thankful as he'd get two weeks in Dubai.

Against Norwich, I was running with Emiliano Buendía, while on a yellow and he leaned into me, then went forward. They were counter-attacking and it looked to the ref like I'd dragged him down.

I played a dangerous game at times, some borderline tackles. It was regularly said that if I got a yellow, my style of play would be impacted, but I'd disagree with that. I wasn't an idiot… I knew when I could put in a tackle.

I always felt in control.

I WAS SUSPENDED for three games after playing Portsmouth, all the time wondering how much of a price I would pay? Then Cattermole got injured the day before facing Man City.

Suddenly, I was back in the team.

A huge home game. It was the early days of the money flowing into Man City. Roberto Mancini was manager… Carlos Tevez up front, Vincent Kompany at the back. Shay Given was in goal.

I enjoyed the midfield battle. They started with Gareth Barry and Nigel De Jong, and brought on Patrick Vieira. Myself and Steed Malbranque dug in for the fight. It finished 1-1… a sickener, as Adam Johnson levelled with a great strike in the last minute. But the game went well for me.

I had a clash with Barry at one stage.

I went in hard in a tackle… he jumped up and started yapping away.

'WHO YOU TACKLING LIKE THAT… YOU'RE UGLY!'

Gareth's trash-talking needed some work. My attitude was to get noticed again. The fans recognised the effort and the reception was unreal. It was hard to believe they were the same group that had been hammering me.

Steed Malbranque was an incredible player to be alongside at Sunderland. I played with him for a few seasons in the Premier League. He'd a great career getting to play for so long with Tottenham and Fulham in England, along with Lyon in France. Always performed in midfield, whether it be in the middle, either wing or at No 10.

Nothing too flash or fancy, he just worked extremely hard and was super fit. Creative with his passing as well… could control a ball in a phone box. You'd never get the ball off him. An ideal teammate and I benefitted from playing alongside him in midfield.

We'd some good moments together.

He was quiet, but a really nice guy… never groaned or moaned. Didn't smile or laugh much either. There was only one occasion, my first year there, when we'd a Christmas night out. We were sitting down having dinner in Manchester and Steed was moaning that his arms were sore.

I just happened to be sitting alongside him as he was giving out.

'I'm a footballer, not some weight-lifter!'

Everyone was so surprised, it was the first time we'd ever heard him giving out.

But then again, we'd all had a couple drinks and it was a rare lapse from him in his character. He had huge talent and was a really good professional.

I'd say he was a manager's dream.

I WAS MAKING progress and April 2010 was when it felt like everything came together. One of those perfect phases that footballers are searching for. Four games in the space of three weeks. I started them all; we won three.

First up… Tottenham.

One of the best Saturday afternoons of my career. The Stadium of Light was packed for a 3pm kick-off; the place bouncing from the start, as the energy rolled off the stands and down onto the pitch. Harry Redknapp had brought Tottenham to town. He had Bale and Modric in his midfield running the show, and chasing a Champions League place. They got over that line a few weeks later, but first we knocked them back a couple of strides.

It was a crazy match.

Darren Bent was fired up for it against the club he'd left the previous summer. He scored in the first minute, and then again from a penalty after a half hour. The madness started as we tried to kill the game.

Bent had another penalty before half-time saved by Heurelho Gomes. Then, into the second-half, I'm through on the right of the box and Wilson Palacios clips me. Another Bent chance for the hat-trick… another penalty miss as Gomes saves. A few minutes later Anton Ferdinand has a goal ruled out for a foul.

It looked like we were going to pay when they brought on Peter Crouch and he headed in a Modric cross with 20 minutes left. But we did finish them off… Boudewijn Zenden volleying in a screamer for a 3-1 win.

There is no better place than Sunderland on a day like that. The fans were walking on air and further good results rewarded the love they had for their club. There was no heart-stopping last day of the season… we were safe by then.

After the win at Hull to round off April, I got drug tested after the game. Dad waited for me and we drove back to Sunderland together. The journey home took four hours. At the time Hull was alien to us, we didn't have a clue where we were going. The two of us didn't care.

We were on cloud nine. I was a month off my 21st birthday, into my second season in England and I felt I was starting to arrive in the Premier League.

There were just two games left in the season... against Manchester United and Wolves. And then everything changed.

THERE IS A before, and after story, in my career and it hinges on one day... May 2, 2010.

Second last game of the Premier League season with Sunderland. My first time playing Manchester United and the excitement was high.

Only two years since they'd won the Champions League in Moscow and they still had a team of stars. The football-mad youngster in me couldn't wait to have a go at playing against Scholes, Giggs and Rooney.

Just before the half-hour mark, Nani put them ahead. Then just after the half-hour mark, the ball broke to Patrice Evra. I charged towards him.

He leaned across and I got knocked off my stride. That's when my knee buckled; went into spasm and felt momentarily numb. The pain was bearable. *Take a couple minutes, get to the sideline, shake it off... and go again.*

The medics came rushing in... Sunderland physio Pete Brand and the doctor Glen Rae. They examined my knee. They instantly diagnosed a damaged cruciate and a stretcher was needed

I was taken off and into a physio room, looking at the bag of ice covering my knee. A few of the Sunderland subs came in to see how I was... Steve Bruce popped his head in at half-time. The team still had a game to play.

That had to be the focus... no room for sentimentality.

I was alone with my thoughts. The career-turning nature of that day didn't register at the time. I couldn't compute this was a long-term injury, even though I could hear the 'cruciate talk' and that a scan was needed.

Only when I later met the surgeon did the bad news really hit home.

IT WAS A Bank Holiday weekend in England, so the scan results didn't come back until Tuesday. They sketched out the mess my knee was in.

All the ligaments... cruciate, lateral, medial... were destroyed.

Bone ripped from my knee-cap. The bicep femoris tendon that connects the hamstring to the knee had been snapped off.

The initial thinking was that my career was done.

Get set for retirement.

The world had seemed to be at my feet with first-team appearances… the offer by Sunderland of a new five-year contract and speculation I was going to get an Ireland senior call-up.

One tackle later, and I'm facing the prospect of my playing days being over.

What the hell is going to happen now?

BY THE END of that week, I went under the knife to repair the damage. The surgeon was Dr Steve Bollen, based in Bradford. He had an arrogant attitude in talking about his work. I didn't mind that. He bragged he was the best and said he could fix me. He was worried if I'd do the necessary rehab to recover.

I was worried he'd do the surgery properly.

We disagreed, but I stressed that I'd do what I was told.

The operation was at 9am in Bradford, about two hours from where I lived. Sunderland put on a driver for me… the plan was I would be collected at 6.30am. Having to fast from midnight, I wolfed down a big dinner at five minutes to 12 to ease off the hunger in the morning.

Then I slept-in.

Dick was my chauffeur for the day, a lovely man who had to bang my door down for about 20 minutes to waken me up. When we landed, the surgeon was standing outside with his scrubs and gloves on, shouting… 'COME ON!'

Dave Binningsley was the physio assigned to my recovery. He watched the surgery so he'd be there when I woke up. He told me later that when the surgeon finished stitching up, he took his gloves off, and went 'JORDAN'… mimicking a basketball shot as he tossed them into the bin.

But he was delighted with how the work went. It would be 18 months before I was back in football due to the extent of the injury I had suffered.

I did the sums in my head.

That was all of the 2010-11 season gone.

I'd turn 22 in May 2011… figured I'd aim to be back for a full pre-season after that summer. Every players starts that 'game' when they get injured.

How much time can I knock off this?

Everyone's looking for cuts.

Maybe I could shave another six months off…get it down to a year!

It was a testament to Steve Bruce how he acted after. I was back at the training ground on crutches and he came to see me.

'We'll give you the contract… there's no problem.'

I'd wondered were they going to back out? Those doubts were natural when the suggestion was made that I should retire. So, I was very grateful to him for pushing that through and the club for looking after me. It put my mind at ease.

The rehab plan was to work in 12-week blocks and return for a check-up after each.

I needed to do everything in my power to get back.

JOHN O'SHEA HAD been centre-half for Manchester United in the game and had come to see me after in the physio room that day. We had a five-minute chat… he wished me all the best. I'd never met him before.

It was an older Waterford lad checking in with a young Cork fella, but really how many opposition players would have done that? I'm not sure it would have crossed my mind straight after a match.

John went out of his way to meet me. It was a really nice gesture. We didn't know at the time we'd become Sunderland teammates a year later or go on to have experiences together with Ireland. John is the best sort of person you could aspire to be, with the type of standards by which he lives his life.

When himself and Wes Brown joined Sunderland in July 2011, I was doing rehab for my second cruciate on the day they had their medical at the training ground. At the start I was almost in awe of them, these multi-Premier League winners that were suddenly in our dressing-room. Training with them every day, you got to see their high standards and understand why they'd lasted so long at Manchester United. For all the profile the sport had given them, they were just normal, hard-working lads.

AFTER I TORE the cruciate, I got another call of support. It was a surprise to hear the voice on the other end.

'David, it's Roy here!'

I grew up admiring Roy Keane so much, and here he was being generous with his time and kind with his words. He talked about knuckling down for rehab, trusting the surgeon and physio… not to get side-tracked from the target I was aiming for… not to fall out of the team circle and… not to wake up one morning feeling sorry for myself and fall behind.

Roy also got in touch just to see how I was?

He helped realign my thinking. He understood from his own injury experiences and knew the thoughts that could consume someone's mind at that time. His view was if he could recover, I could.

That message helped shape my attitude. Roy is someone you listen to.

THE INNOCENCE OF youth.

It helped that I was 21 when I tore my cruciate and didn't have another care in the world. Contrast that to when I had a shoulder surgery a week before my wife had a C-section when Brody was born. In the hospital, the mid-wife turned to me but I wasn't able to hold him… my arm was in a sling. At 29, married with two children, there was a lot more going on during that injury recovery.

When I was younger facing rehab, I was more carefree. And not engulfed by doubt. I had that bit of fearlessness.

What do I need to do to get back?

This was another obstacle in my way to playing in the Premier League. Injury can cause mental health struggles but I was fortunate it didn't get on top of me.

I kept in touch with the first-team… always kept 10.30am-12pm free so I could watch the lads train and not feel isolated from the group. I went to all the home games and any away fixtures that were within two hours. The club was happy to facilitate that.

I did my cruciate in May, then Frazier Campbell did his in August. As bleak as it sounds, maybe there was an element of fortune in that. We were in it together. In a freak occurrence, we both did two cruciates back-to-back. During tough days in rehab, there was someone to lean on for support and drive one another on.

We also had Dave. When you're injured, the physio becomes your best friend.

He's now first-team physio at Man United; we still speak regularly.

I had a massive metal brace on my knee after the operation and needed to do some work in the swimming pool to get my muscles moving. It took me an hour to take my first step. I couldn't bring myself to put my weight on the leg. I had a complete mental block.

Dave was great, he didn't push me, told me to do it in my own time. All that help was great but it mainly comes down to the individual's attitude and I didn't see any reason why I couldn't get back.

Johnny Small, as I say, was a friend of Jordan Henderson's. He was in a university course that didn't interest him much and was happy to help out any way he could. I couldn't drive for three months, so I got him insured on my car.

He drove me anywhere I needed to go around Sunderland. His mother Julie cooked dinners for me... she washed my clothes. The amount that his mum, and his dad Duncan, and that family did for me was incredible.

AS MUCH AS I was determined to return, there was naturally doubt about whether I would be the same player again? In a way, I never was.

I lost a yard of pace; I was a lot quicker when I was younger. I tailored my game, though I loved tackling... the art of it. As I got older, I just needed to learn to read the game. Pick up pockets of space and look to intercept passes. Get a better grasp of what would make me a good defensive midfielder instead of playing off the cuff.

After a summer of hard work, I was buzzing for the 2010-11 season. Around September, I felt I was moving better. Bruce and the physio did point out I was running lopsided, not putting proper weight through my leg, but I corrected that. Physios and doctors were happy.

It was just a matter of ticking the boxes... non-contact training, contact training, a reserve game... then try to get into the first-team. I was known for my tackling but the club fined me £50 every time I went in for a slide-tackle at training. They wanted me to stay on my feet as I recovered, so Bruce came up with that fine system.

It had been a positive start to the season for the club.

We were in the top six on Christmas Day. A 5-1 defeat away to Newcastle was a disaster but results like beating Chelsea 3-0 at Stamford Bridge were huge.

I played some reserve games in November and then the first-team came calling. A start in mid-December away to Fulham.

I didn't feel great beforehand. Reserve games are nothing fixtures… this was the Premier League. Fulham players rightly had no regard for the state of my fitness. They were there to beat us.

How would I cope in that environment?

I played just under an hour and survived.

Asamoah Gyan replaced me, our big-money signing who had starred for Ghana in the World Cup. We drew 0-0 and two weeks later, I got to realise my nan's target of playing at Old Trafford.

I'm not into the element of hatred amongst football fans. I grew up a Liverpool fan and understand the heated rivalry with Manchester United, but I still admired the club. Playing in their stadium was a big deal. My nan loved Alex Ferguson and his older team with Bruce and Pallister at the back.

We lost 2-0, but it still felt like a significant day.

BY JANUARY 2011 I was back in a familiar place. In Bradford, with a busted knee, to see Steve Bollen. He quickly pointed out the recurrence was no reflection on his initial surgery work. I accepted that.

After that night in Villa Park, I had moments thinking my knee didn't feel as bad as the first time. There was a slight cruciate tear, the right knee again. It needed surgery but it wasn't snapped. The surgeon's original work had been so good that it didn't all come apart and he was confident that I'd be okay.

Back to rehab work with Dave.

I had greater insight into what was required but the frustration was deeper. All the exercises you do are new the first time, but feel repetitive the second time. I'd always say to someone who's done their knee that the sooner you can accept this is a long journey, the sooner you will get back playing. Dwelling on why it happened, as natural as that is, won't help you one bit.

The work has to be done.

After Liverpool won the Champions League final in 2019, I was at the after-party and got talking to Alex Oxlade-Chamberlain. I made a point of congratulating him, not on the victory but on having made it back into the squad, a year after he'd damaged his knee so badly against Roma.

There is a sort of 'Cruciate Club', a sense of brotherhood amongst those who endure the injury. There we were on one of the biggest nights of his career, trading war stories on injuries.

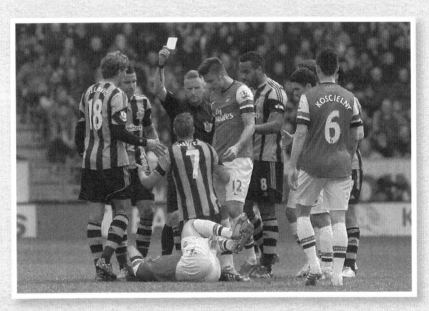

I knew my role on the field, and that was as a combative midfielder to begin with, fighting for possession and laying the ball off to others... and taking punishment was part of that job (above on the receiving end of the referee against Arsenal). It's not that surprising I was so unfortunate with injuries.

When Tigers Roared

STEVE BRUCE IS a really good man-manager. He could assess what the team needed. At the end of November, we lost to Crystal Palace but were still allowed our pre-arranged Christmas party. We flew to Dublin that night; out on the Sunday in Temple Bar with Monday off.

Back to work on Tuesday, we felt refreshed and knuckled down. Next up was Liverpool at home.

The day before the game, Bruce asked me was I ready to play? I nodded.

'You'd better be clean-shaven then!'

I took no chances, went home and got rid of the beard. I didn't understand his motivation but took no chances. He told me years later that they'd an FA Cup final with Man United and as they boarded the bus, Ferguson had demanded to know why one player wasn't clean-shaven? That player was a bag of nerves but the incident stopped him getting overawed by the game.

I didn't think I was nervous like that, yet it felt like a little trick by Bruce to distract me from thinking too much about facing Suarez, Gerrard, Sterling and the rest on the Sunday.

Liverpool pushed hard for the title that season.

They only lost six games, but one of them was to us. The match was a dream. I set up Livermore for the first, scored the second and we won 3-1. Afterwards, I had this superstition for a while about shaving before every game.

It was my first time playing Liverpool, the club I grew up supporting, but I didn't get caught up in that sideshow. Emotion and friendships were pushed aside. Jordan got the ball at one stage and I nailed him. He moaned at me for a few weeks after as he'd damaged his ankle. But we're all professional.

Once the whistle is blown, no one cares who they know.

That Liverpool game was a reminder of how special Hull home games could be. The place was alive.

And I produced a moment that contributed to that.

In the 72nd minute, there was a scramble for the ball and it broke on the edge of the box. I whacked in a shot. Blocked... but I got a second chance from the rebound. I took a touch with my right, and moved to my left... steadied for a moment.

And pulled the trigger again.

Often, I'm so focused on technique using my left foot, that I lose balance. As I shot, I fell over and it was only hearing the screams a second later that confirmed the ball was in the back of the net. I got up, and ran around in a state of shock.

First Premier League goal... we were in front 2-1.

IT WAS ONE of the best days.

My second arrived later that month against Man United.

Sometime later, I was at Liverpool visiting Jordan. He'd training so I went in to watch and he sent me upstairs to the canteen for breakfast. Brendan Rodgers walked in and did a double-take when he saw me; then came over to say hello and sat down for a chat.

He brought up that game against us, and marked it as a turning point in their season. All the talk later was how the title challenge came apart in the loss to Chelsea, when Steven Gerrard slipped, and the draw with Crystal Palace. But Rodgers went back to their defeat to us... that was the type of game they couldn't afford to lose if they were to become champions.

I always felt comfortable in front of goal. Clearcut chances didn't come often but when they did, I didn't panic. I always felt I could outsmart the goalkeeper. That's a key part of it.

Goalscoring was not central to my game, but I hit four that season, all significant. Two in the league and two in the FA Cup.

Steve Bruce would point out it'd be great if I could score in the regular matches instead of saving them for the big games.

In the FA quarter-final that year against Sunderland, I came inside on my left when the expectancy would have been I'd hit it with my right. I had blocked down Lee Cattermole, the pitch opened up and after sprinting from my own box, I just needed to keep my head. In the semi-final against Sheffield United, I shot high to the net as the goalkeeper dived low. I felt composed in those situations. I ended up taking penalties in my last season with Hull for that reason.

Cup runs are a great distraction. That spring, it felt like a release from the pressure of trying to avoid relegation. We felt confident playing Sunderland after doing the double over them in the league.

The semi-final against Sheffield United at Wembley was bigger. A crazy game to play in… eight goals, the first-half shambolic.

Yannick Sagbo put us in front, but we were complacent against a League One team and Sheffield hit two to go ahead. Steve Bruce said nothing at the break, but Curtis Davies went berserk, grabbing players, throwing fellas against the wall… the whole lot. He was captain, screaming about the importance of getting to an FA Cup final.

We took over in the second-half.

Matty Fryatt, Quinny and Huddlestone all scored… 4-2 up by the 67th minute and we were cruising. They scored in the 90th minute… 4-3.

A little doubt started to creep in… 71,820 people watching on.

I passed to Matty, and went again.

He hit it wide to Elmohamady.

I could hear Bruce roaring.

'TAKE IT TO THE CORNER!'

'TAKE IT TO THE F***ING CORNER!'

It's understandable. But I've run on, looked around. The Sheffield United defence was stretched; I'd a clear path to goal. If it was anyone else on that pitch other than Elmo, they wouldn't have made that pass.

We'd been at Sunderland together and then Hull. I've never played with anyone more often. I scream and he puts me in… took a touch with my left, chose where to put it with my right.

TV commentator: *That'll do it. A fifth goal for Hull City, who are heading to their first ever FA Cup final.*

The relief washed over me.

I jogged slowly over to the fans… drained but elated.

WHAT THE HELL is Alan Pardew doing?

That's the first thought that entered my head.

We're losing 3-1 to Newcastle. The ball goes out over the touchline. I race to get it. Pardew goes to put his foot on the ball and then pulls it away.

That annoys me… we start shouting at each other. Then I think he felt we were going head-to-head. He makes a move forward. It's not a proper headbutt, but I'm not happy. Elmo tries to calm me down.

Loads of players wade in.

The referee Kevin Friend gives me a yellow for retaliation and Pardew is sent to the stand; later he gets slapped with a seven-game ban. Newcastle end up winning 4-1 and afterwards that's the biggest talking point… we'd been pumped at home.

But the Pardew story explodes and the impact still lingers. During lockdown in 2020 when all of sport was shut down, I was reminded of it on TV one day.

Ten Most Bizarre Moments In Premier League History.

It makes the cut.

It was a weird time. Steve and my dad both said the same thing after… stay away from the media. Everyone tried to get me for an interview, to hear my side of the story. It was a long time before I spoke about it.

I didn't care too much. He hadn't hurt me or knocked me over. That would have been embarrassing… at least I stood my ground. The loss concerned me more, as we headed on international break with Ireland. Everyone there wanted to talk about it. Pardew wouldn't be the most liked figure, and there were plenty of suggestions I should have hit back. But I never thought that was the wisest move.

On the Monday after, I got a phone call. The police wanted to discuss the incident.

I hung up.

They tried again… I hung up again.

I was convinced it was one of the Hull lads winding me up. The club secretary rang and said it was a serious call; the police needed to know if I wanted to press charges. I'd no interest going down that road.

Pardew never apologised in person or contacted me himself after. It was bad form that he didn't just ring me to clear the air and admit he'd lost his cool for a moment.

The club received some token letter which he'd signed, but I never looked at it. We played Crystal Palace later when he was their manager. In the tunnel before the match, I went to shake his hand and kept looking at him. He shook my hand, said nothing and just turned away.

He'll never forget me for the rest of his life after that incident. He had the opportunity that day to say, 'Sorry about all that'.

Just acknowledge it.

But he didn't and that was his call.

THE 1996 FINAL is my first memory of the FA Cup... Eric Cantona hitting the late winner, the Liverpool players in their white suits. It is a special competition and I had a chance to win it in 2014. It was a magical cup run for the players, and the fans and everyone connected with the club. Cup runs are a great distraction.

That spring, it felt like a release from the pressure of trying to stay away from the bottom of the table. From the start of March, we lost eight of our last 11 Premier League games. Our form wasn't great but we kept progressing in the FA Cup and it was a buzz that kept the squad going.

It started off up in Middlesbrough in January with a 2-0 win in the third round, Aaron McClean and Nick Proschwitz scoring in either half.

Then another 2-0 win on the road; Matty Fryatt scoring twice in the second-half to make sure we had a good trip to Southend in the fourth round.

We needed two attempts before beating Brighton, 1-1 down at their place for a draw after Yannick Sagbo saved us in the 86th minute with his equalizer. We grabbed the second chance to win 2-1 at home in the replay; Curtis Davies and Robert Koren got the goals.

The importance and the pressure of the games started to grow but we lived up to the expectations... the quarter-final at home to Sunderland and the semi-final at Wembley against Sheffield United.

Hull City in the FA Cup final.

But first I was fearful I might miss it.

After playing Man United a couple weeks earlier, I was accused of stamping on Adnan Januzaj. It turned into a big storm but I hadn't meant to stamp on him. Steve Bruce fought tooth and nail that it wasn't intentional. A three-match ban would have meant I'd miss the final. He left me out for a game against Everton, shielded me from the attention.

There was a pile-on from United fans, but I stayed clear of that and escaped any suspension.

The build-up in Hull to the cup final was huge; this enormous sporting occasion that the whole city bought into. We got the train to London the night before and went to our hotel. The mood was relaxed... a few of us played Fifa that night, and I felt good the next morning going for a walk.

My pre-match meal plan was Weetabix in the morning, then later... chicken, pasta and bolognese sauce. That day I was one of the last to queue... there was no chicken left. I was giving out that all the food was gone... the fitness coach got stressed out but it didn't matter much in the end. My reaction was just a sign of big-game nerves.

Then, upstairs to get ready and put on the cup final suit... and ushered onto a bus. As we turned up Wembley Way, it was two hours before kick-off with only a bunch of fans there. Later the pubs would spill out the thousands going to the game.

We arrived, and after a while Bruce brought in a guest to the changing room... David Beckham. It was a genius move. Beckham came in, and just popped around the room to meet everyone. It was a good distraction.

Some of the lads who didn't make the squad grabbed him for selfies.

Every game in that cup run, we'd been above the team we were facing in the league. We always felt we should win. The difference now was the opposition. With Arsenal, we said we *could* win.

We were so well drilled; knew exactly what we were doing. We lined up in the tunnel together... Arsenal came out in dribs and drabs, lads hadn't their laces tied... were slow putting their shirts on. A few high-fived the referee.

Not sure they're tuned in.

We were staring out at that pitch and waiting for that first whistle. That's why the game started the way it did.

Firstly, Quinny arrows a corner to Tom at the edge of the box. He fires a shot in at pace and Chester just diverts it to the far corner of the net.

Then a cross comes in from deep and I almost get ahead of Bacary Sagna to head it, but it flies just past us. Quinny makes space and stands up a cross. Alex Bruce gets a header in… hits the post and Curtis smashes in the rebound.

Eight minutes gone in the FA Cup final. We're winning 2-0 because two of our three centre-halves have scored.

What's happening?

WE'D BEEN HERE before. It's not the first time Chester has scored in the fourth minute that season; same story at home to Man United back in December. The class of Man United told that day as they won 3-2.

And the class of Arsenal also eventually told.

If we'd survived until half-time with that 2-0 lead, I feel I'd have got my hands on that trophy after the game. But Santi Cazorla put a free-kick in the top corner… 2-1 at the break. We needed another goal but didn't want to commit too many forward. There was danger in their team everywhere you looked… Arteta, Ramsey, Cazorla, Özil, Podolski and Giroud all starting.

Koscielny scores and it goes to extra-time. I could sense trouble.

Our bodies are tired now, our minds just hoping we get to penalties. They throw on Rosicky and Wilshere. *We're wrecked.* It's the only game I've ever got cramp in. Running down the wing after over 110 minutes, with 16km in the bank… my left calf locks.

If it had gone to a shootout, I'm not sure I'd have had the energy for the walk from the centre circle to size up the kick. It didn't get that far… Ramsey buries the third goal and Arsenal are ahead.

We've poured our heart and soul into it, but that's the winner.

Straight after game, I got drug tested. Drained and dehydrated, I just couldn't give the testers the sample they wanted so we could all go home.

The game kicked off at 5pm. There was a post-match event organised for players and families at 8.30pm; I didn't get there until two and a half hours later. My family were waiting but I was so frustrated after the day I didn't want to go to the party and just went straight to my room. Dad came up to me.

Be with the rest of the lads. No point wallowing on your own.

That was his message!

ALL MY BUDDIES landed at the hotel, the gang from Cork I grew up with… all wearing the Hull shirts they'd put on for the day. We sorted entry for them all.

Niall Quinn was there, he's good mates with Bruce. He came over to our Irish group, sat down and had a few pints. The lads were desperate to get Niall to sing, and he joined in a couple of times when the lads started.

And it actually turned into a nice night, with plenty of people around to help ease the disappointment of the loss

I was heartbroken at the time but can now appreciate the incredible occasion it was. If we'd lost to Sheffield United, I'd have lived with that regret for the rest of my life. Against Arsenal, we gave it everything but just came up short facing a good team.

Dad used to reflect a lot then over how far I'd come. From being trapped in a tunnel trying to get my knee right, that was the season I moved into the light.

FA Cup run.

Goals against big teams.

Constant games.

Staying in the Premier League.

A great adventure from start to finish.

Playing against Liverpool (top), the team I followed as a young lad was something special for me. And 'What's Alan Pardew doing?' was my first thought before he and I had a moment on the sideline which has unfortunately gone down in football TV history.

A FATHER'S VIEW

'IN A WAY, I would be mad jealous of my son

'David played soccer for 13 years in England and got paid for it. I would have loved the opportunity to play hurling for 13 years and get paid for it. To have sport at the centre of your life, being rewarded financially as a result and to then retire after with the support of a lovely family.

'I am proud of what David has done. He moved to England in July 2008 and retired from playing there in August 2019. Over that time, I travelled over to be at 85%-to-90% of the games he played. He always knew I would be at his games.

'I would message to say I wanted one ticket; a handful of times I needed more if I had someone with me. David always sorted that out. Stella often came to games and she made a trip out of it for a few days. Sarah came on other occasions, but I mostly went on my own.

'I was happy to make that journey over and back in a day, sticking to my routine. For Saturday 3pm kick-offs, the alarm went off at home at 5am... get up and go to Cork airport. I flew most often to Manchester; it was two hours from Hull for home games and within easy reach of plenty of other venues around north-west England for away games.

'Picked up the car at the airport I'd hired the previous week, and away I went. Premier League games with Hull sometimes meant flights to London and a jump on the Underground to reach a stadium. If I needed more flight options, I would drive to Dublin on a Saturday morning and could be heading over to Leeds-Bradford or Newcastle.

'Landing at the stadium meant a chance to park up and catch up on some sleep in the car. Team buses arrived around 2pm and I'd always be there to salute David. Head to the ticket office at every ground, pick up the envelope left for me under his name and then go in to take my seat for the match. I was very organised, constantly checking the match schedules for Sunderland or later Hull, and working out my plans a few weeks in advance.

'The success of the trips hinged on how the match went for David. In 2015, Hull were away to Brighton in the Championship. David started poorly in midfield and was taken off after half an hour. The red card in Fratton Park coming on against Portsmouth in 2010 was another day to forget. But those low moments were rare. His effort levels and application were consistently good, his performances were worth travelling to witness.

'Some people thought I was mad. But my presence over there was not to pressurise him or criticise him. I wanted to be there for David. We always met after the match, chatted for a few minutes. I'd ask him did he need anything and then would throw in a couple comments about the game.

'SOME DAYS WERE destined never to be forgotten.

When Hull were at home to Liverpool in December 2013, I brought a buddy over with me, Colin Harris. He'd hurled for me when I was manager of Kerry and Kilmoyley.

'Colin was a big Liverpool fan. He'd picked out that game once Hull got promoted to the Premier League and booked his place as my travel companion.

'The stadium was full and rocking from the start that day. We were sitting behind the goal when David scored at the opposite end to put Hull ahead during the second-half. The place erupted and the fans sang all the way to the end of the 3-1 victory. Everyone was on a high after when we went into the players' lounge.

'Colin was a bit sore seeing Liverpool lose but he soon got over it. David gave him Jordan Henderson's jersey as they'd swapped after the match.

'I loved that hour after the game, moving around this place I had special access to, mingling with Premier League stars and the Hull staff for the match post-mortem over a sandwich and cup of tea.

'There was a big Irish contingent at Hull and we got to know all their families. Stephen Quinn's brothers were regulars, the same with Paul McShane's family. Robbie Brady's dad and his brother. They weren't all there as much as me but we became a group, often meeting up after the game.

'Steve Bruce was a huge figure in David's career, the manager he played under the most. I met Bruce all the time, had many great conversations with him. The meetings tended to be at Hull's training ground; I didn't want to bother him on match day.

'An absolute gentleman.

'Mike Phelan was assistant manager to Bruce for a while and then later became manager. Mike was mad interested in hurling, through his father being a Kilkenny native, and was always keen to meet and chat about that.

'In September 2018, David got me involved in a charity match... Liverpool and Celtic in Glasgow. My role for the day was assistant manager to Jurgen Klopp. A fascinating experience. I was Cork manager at the time and Klopp was really keen to ask questions about hurling...the speed of it, the tactics, the approach to matches. In return, I got an insight into his work as a manager.

'It was brilliant, a lot of sportspeople are really genuine.

'The high-profile characters in English soccer command the attention but there is a whole group of people fuelling the engine that drives the club. The staff at Hull were wonderful; the security guys dotted around the stadium on match day were so sound to deal with. They reminded me of the late Tommy Lynch, who was stadium caretaker of Páirc Uí Chaoimh and Páirc Uí Rinn for many years.

'These are the people in the soul of a sports club or team who are hugely important to the players. And the people in those roles at Hull and Sunderland were really important figures in David's life.

'THE TRAVEL WASN'T all glamour. I'll never forget a midweek night in 2008 in Morecambe, a Lancashire town on the west coast of England.

'Sunderland were playing a reserve match against Everton, not long after David had signed for the club. Back then, the best way for me to travel over was on the boat from Dublin to Holyhead, something I often later did for midweek games.

'When I landed that day, David rang to say the venue for the game had been changed from the Liverpool area. The only issue was they didn't know where it had been switched to. I was talking away to him and next thing I see the lights flashing behind me; the police pull me over on the motorway.

'I pleaded my case.

'I'm really sorry, but it's an emergency.'

'What's the emergency?'

'My son is playing a match for Sunderland and he's ringing, trying to tell me where it has been changed. Look, just let me off this time... I won't be on the phone again.'

'Well won't you have to be on phone when he rings to say where the match is on?' We got a good laugh out of that but I was let off, promising to pull in to take the call when David rang. Eventually the game was fixed for Morecambe, a three-hour drive north from Holyhead. I made it with five minutes to spare before kick- off to be greeted by a mixture of snow and rain blowing across the pitch.

'Reserve matches started at 7pm; David would emerge out after by 9pm and, after a quick chat, I'd to dash back to make the boat sailing at half two in the morning. There was a McDonalds in North Wales which was my frequent pitstop... my goal always was to get there before closing time of 11pm to grab some dinner.

'Travelling on winter nights meant you were at the mercy of the weather, waiting for the road closures that would send you off on a tour. I bought a Sat Nav, my trusted companion for those journeys that helped me out when heading down small roads in Wales, keeping one eye on the clock and trying to make the boat home.

'I FELT A savage pride at watching David play at Hull in a period where the club was really progressing. Over time, he became part of the fabric of the club and I could see the fans responding to that. Hull was where I got to know people best, as invariably I'd be sitting in the same section, week after week.

'There was a game at Anfield when a Hull fan roared at him from the first minute to last. I never got involved in those situations.

'Stay restrained, don't bite back.

'The minute you open your mouth, the Irish accent is a giveaway and they'll make the family connection. It's not going to be a positive outcome. There were times when Stella and Sarah were with me; they got offended and found it harder to take.

'But it drove me harder to do everything in my power to make sure David settled in England to his new way of life. It helped that David was driven. When he joined Sunderland, I told him that he should thank Roy for bringing him to England. He did, but Roy didn't want to receive any gratitude.

'I did nothing. You brought yourself to England.

'Now it's up to you to stay here.'

'LATER, THE TRAVEL was not just over to England.

We were on the international stage, heading to Dublin and all over Europe as David started to nail down a place in the Ireland squad. I still get goosebumps watching replays of the John O'Shea goal against Germany in 2014. Last kick of the game on his 100th cap to secure a draw and David had played the whole match after filling a gap at right-back.

'It was amazing to get your head around it.

'The layout of the stadium at Gelsenkirchen had the dressing-rooms locked away. I rang him and he came back out onto the pitch to see myself and Stella up in the stand. We drove to Amsterdam after and were in a hotel for a few hours before the next morning's flight. I was wired with adrenaline after the game, and sat in the room at 3am with a can of Heineken to toast the result.

'Cardiff in October 2017 was better again.

'That is my highlight of David's career. Without question.

'I didn't lack company that Monday night. Stella, Sarah and her partner Eugene were all on the flight over. David was captain of his country and a World Cup play-off spot was on the line. No one was going to miss it.

'There was a huge sense of anticipation in the city during the day. Fans always have some nerves on match day but when your son is playing, there's that extra emotion. Over the years I learned to control that, not to get anxious and trusted that David was capable of performing.

'I used to get asked what was my priority... the team to win or David to play well? I always said to get the win first and then we could rate his display. A team victory would always help cushion a personal blow, we both agreed on that. Even when he did his cruciate for the second time, we took consolation from Sunderland's 1-0 win that night.

'The Cardiff City stadium was packed by kick-off. When they belted out the Welsh national anthem, *Land of my Fathers* beforehand, the level of noise whipped up was absolutely frightening. The hairs were standing on the back of my neck as I looked around the stadium and I could feel this raw desperation in the air with everybody wanting so badly to go to Russia the following summer.

'When James McClean scored in the second-half, we nearly lost our lives.

'Total bedlam.

'We were sitting in the middle, near the tunnel where the players come out. All the families of the Irish players were together, that was always the way. These were the people you celebrated and commiserated with; James' family were right in front of us, it was such a moment of pure joy for them.

'Shane Long's mother was always there; the same for her when he scored against Germany in 2015. When Robbie Brady hit the winner against Italy in Euro 2016 in Lille, his dad Shay was roaring up at me after... "That's my son there, John!"

'We were all the same.

'Parents incredibly proud to see our children representing their country. South-East Radio in Wexford rang early the next morning; Alan Corcoran had me on for a half hour as the proud father providing the eyewitness account from Ireland's win over Wales.

'A night I will never forget.

'THERE WERE TIMES I worried about David. Any parent, when their child moves abroad, you hope they'll get on okay. If they're a professional soccer player who destroys his knee twice, that concern is increased.

'In those moments it was a comfort for us back in Cork to know there were people looking out for David in Sunderland.

'Before the Euros started in 2021, Liverpool released a video on social media to commemorate Jordan Henderson's decade at the club. His dad Brian was talking about his son's career. That's the Brian Henderson I knew from the start... a terrific person, very good in looking out for people.

'He gave David great help when he was making his way at Sunderland, always on the end of the phone if we needed him. If ever I wasn't sure how he was doing, I could ask Brian to check up on him. He'd come back to say they'd met up or all gone for dinner and everything was fine. Brian was a really genuine person.

'Jordan's friends pitched in. Johnny Small was David's chauffeur, the staff at the Toby pub nearby kept him fed. He's blessed with the friends he's had... he's still close to that Sunderland crew, and it's the same when he comes back to Cork. I still see him knocking around with the lads he grew up with.

'I always believed he would recover from the injuries. I just wanted us to get a break, that's what I prayed for; a clear run for David where he was fit and could show everyone how he could perform.

'In May 2014, we reached the type of day I'd dreamed about.

'I grew up in an era when the FA Cup final was a huge sporting event, along with the Grand National and All-Ireland finals; those were the main occasions where we huddled around the TV in our home in Wexford.

'The 1965 final is still clear in my mind when Liverpool beat Leeds United 2-1. Almost half a century later, I watched my son walk out from the Wembley tunnel to play in a game of that importance. The stadium was packed and the place felt alive.

'It was one of the best moments of my life.'

Still Roaring

WHEN WE LANDED home after the Euros in 2016, I got off in Dublin airport and headed through passport control. Then a BMW came to the runway and spun me over to the Ryanair flight to Portugal that was kept waiting for me. Cally booked our family holiday that summer, but I hadn't checked the dates.

So, when we reached the last 16, I knew I'd to miss the start. After we lost to France, the next day we headed to Ireland as the management were keen for everyone to fly home together.

Someone in the FAI organised the logistics of my trip.

Finally, I got on the plane for Portugal and everyone's staring at the entrance, annoyed and wondering who was delaying the start of their holidays. Luckily, enough people had watched the Euros, so there was a cheer when I boarded. The mood improved, I sat down and we headed off. It was a great trip.

After the play-off final and the summer in France, I needed the break. Especially with the shock I was hit with when we got back. On July 22, Steve Bruce quit as Hull manager. It was a massive personal blow for me. Steve gave me my debut at Sunderland and had brought me to Hull.

I'd describe Steve as my 'father figure' in football… Martin O'Neill is like my 'father-in-law' and Roy Keane is my 'uncle'. I've been very fortunate to have had long relationships with these three people. We'd been on a successful journey at Hull but now it had ended abruptly and the future looked uncertain.

I knew Steve wasn't happy with matters behind the scenes. Frustration was building up. You could tell by his demeanour. After the final win at Wembley, he wasn't in the heart of the celebrations; he seemed restrained.

I've never spoken to Steve about the problems. The Allam family owned the club. I know Steve had a fantastic relationship with the father Assem and a difficult relationship with his son Ehab. I think Ehab had raised questions over the money spent on signings that didn't work out. As we headed to the Premier League, Steve was naturally looking to strengthen his squad. Ehab was getting more involved.

The atmosphere at the club changed.

Compared to our previous promotion in 2013, when we bounced into the new season full of enthusiasm, now there was so much upheaval.

A sorry state of affairs all round.

I'VE NEVER LOST touch with Steve since that time.

Looking from the outside, it was tough to see him going through his messy departure as Newcastle United manager in 2021. It all dragged out and I often wondered how he dealt with it all. Seeing someone I had so much respect and admiration for getting attacked from all different angles is not nice.

Newcastle fans didn't want him and it was becoming a nasty situation.

I have no issue with fan opinions and critical views over a team selection or tactics. The Newcastle fans are a passionate group who love their football. I know that from my time in Sunderland. But with Steve, I felt it got really personal in the stuff thrown at him. A man who had been in the game for so many years was being reduced to the label of a dinosaur who knew nothing about football.

There's no way you last as long in football as he has without knowing what you're doing. By the end, I was just happy for him that he got out of there.

When he left, I said to Cally that he wouldn't stay out of football for too long. It's just in his DNA. So he ended up taking over as West Brom manager in February 2022 and a month later he was heading away to take on Hull. I went to that game and the Hull fans gave him a nice reception at the start.

I've never met a Hull fan speak wrong of him, he's well respected here. Then for the 90 minutes it was a case of game on, Hull fans want to win and Steve was hoping West Brom would.

He got the upper-hand with a 2-0 win that day. After that game I headed down to the West Brom changing room after, had a chat with Steve for 10-15 minutes. It was lovely to catch up. He was more concerned about how I was getting on since retiring as a player, how my coaching plans were going. That's a testament to the person Steve Bruce is.

When he was with Newcastle I would often message him if they had a positive result or things weren't really going his way. Same when he found it tough at West Brom at the start of the new season, and was sacked.

He was very good to me and I have never forgotten that.

IN THE SUMMER of 2014, a new wave of good lads came in to the Hull City squad. Robert Snodgrass was a cheeky fella, a world-class moaner about everything, but with a great personality. He fitted right into our squad.

On deadline day, the Uruguayan striker Abel Hernández and Senegalese midfielder Mo Diamé joined.

Michael Dawson arrived from Spurs.

I couldn't speak highly enough of Michael. A breath of fresh air, an upbeat lad who had time for everyone. He is up there with John O'Shea, Seamus Coleman and Jordan Henderson in terms of leaders I have encountered in my career.

He grew up in North Yorkshire and then moved to Nottingham as a kid to start his football career. Made his first-team breakthrough there, went to Tottenham and became a long-term Premier League regular in their defence. The guy you see now on TV on *Soccer Saturday* every week, is the same as the one that I played with at Hull. Positive, bubbly, always in good form.

Dawson used to land into training every morning after making the drive from his home which was an hour away. I'd be in the physio room and see him bounding in. He'd stop at the door, hang onto the frame above, start stretching his hamstrings and greet everyone in the room.

'Morning! Morning! Morning!' in that booming Yorkshire voice.

You couldn't but be entertained by him. We'd play a game on a Tuesday night and be asking him afterwards, 'Dawson, what are you doing tonight?'

'Oh, gonna head home… sit down now with the wife.

'Watch *Corrie!*

'Get a Chinese!

'Might have two Coronas as well.'

We'd be laughing at him, but he was delighted at the prospect of his *big* night. He was so likeable.

There was a great dynamic there because himself, Livermore and Huddlestone had all played together at Tottenham. They'd all be winding each other up, particularly if Dawson started complaining… the other two would get on his case straightaway.

HARRY MAGUIRE AND Andy Robertson weren't high profile signings. They arrived on the same day at Hull in July 2014; costing around £6 million between them. Harry had been with Sheffield United in League One. Andy was up in Scotland with Dundee United.

It was a stepping-stone for them to bigger things.

Harry becomes Man United captain, reaches a World Cup semi-final and a European Championships final with England. Andy wins the Premier League and Champions League with Liverpool, and helps Scotland reach an international tournament again.

That big time would come later.

When they arrived in Hull they still had to make that jump. Robbo landed in Hull as a young, high-flying full-back. His defending wasn't particularly brilliant at the start but you could see he was destined to improve on it because he wanted to. I often use the example of classing him as a five out of 10 player then. You always felt with time he'd improve.

Going to Liverpool, I thought being alongside those players and working under that manager, he'd go on to a seven or eight and become a brilliant left-back.

But pushing on even further to become now, where I believe he is the best left-back in Europe? I didn't see that coming.

A lot of the performances we see with Liverpool now, there were signs of that with Hull but every aspect of his game has just stepped up. The first man is beaten when he's swinging in a cross… he's the one providing those assists in the team for goals, he's getting into the right position to find the net himself.

The season we got promoted, 2015-16, he played over 50 games for Hull and over 40 of those were in the Championship. It can a long grind of a season, you need lads that are consistently fit and contributing week in, week out. That was Robbo.

He was pivotal that season. The only question after that was could he hit those heights in the Premier League. No bother to him the following year. That got him noticed and Liverpool made their move. He hasn't stopped developing since then. I imagine he's surprised himself a bit. His career has taken off like a rocket.

When we played against Sheffield United in the 2014 FA Cup semi-final, Harry was playing in defence for them. He kept bringing the ball out from the back that day in Wembley, dribbling out to midfield and causing us problems. I'm not sure did that day sway Steve Bruce's thinking, or was Harry on his radar beforehand.

But that game was in April and in July, Harry and Robbo both joined us

The Harry that played for England in the World Cup in 2018 and the Euros in 2021, was very similar to the defender we had in his early days with Hull. He was unfortunate at the start in not getting game-time and was sent out on loan to Wigan. Then he came back and gradually began to play more for Hull, especially when Marco Silva took charge, as he wanted a ball-playing centre-half and Harry was his man. He was excellent in that role and that got him his move to Leicester City.

Harry was always confident in possession. He never really panicked when stepping out from the back. That's stuck with him. I remember at one stage when he was with Leicester, I was watching him play a game and I turned to my dad to say, 'He'll play for England in the World Cup'.

Dad reckoned there was no chance.

But that was the season heading into that tournament in Russia and he just fitted right into what Gareth Southgate wanted. As England manager he had publicly stated he was looking for ball-playing centre-halves. The lad that had joined us from Sheffield United in 2014 hadn't changed, he was perfect for that position.

He's gone through a tough time more recently. As Manchester United have struggled, he's been in the spotlight. Don't get me wrong, he hasn't been fantastic at times and has made mistakes.

But there's been an element of singling him out at a time when United have had plenty of problems and have been a side in decline. Maybe there is something to his position on the pitch... the big, towering centre-half can get the brunt of the criticism. A defender slips up and it can immediately result in a goal.

Their errors are magnified more and get greater attention. Unfortunately, that is part and parcel of football, you have to deal with it. I have felt for him though, because there is a human side to a footballer that is often overlooked.

Steve Bruce was good in his transfer business. He spotted the right characters. He made sure there were very few toxic influences in the dressing-room that might destabilise the squad.

Under Steve Bruce I was very settled at Hull, as I regularly played. There was one period later that some talk emerged of me going to Celtic. Nothing ever materialised.

If it had become a concrete offer, I would have liked to give it a go.

I always had that affection for Celtic growing up. Got Larsson on the back of my first jersey, loved the team that he was the star of, and when I moved to England, I'd regularly go up to Glasgow for matches with one of my mates.

It was a good spin from Hull, over four hours, but I went to all the Champions League home games in 2012. The best was the night Tony Watt scored the famous goal to beat Barcelona. That stadium atmosphere would have been amazing to play in.

I've never lost touch with Steve Bruce, even when he departed Hull. He's a brilliant manager, and someone who was always there to help and guide me through my career.

THE INTERNATIONAL STAGE

INTERNATIONAL FOOTBALL TRAVEL is not glamorous. You're there to do a job. Fly in... get the right result... home!

My first away trip was in October 2012.

A World Cup qualifier in Tórshavn, home of the Faroe Islands. I was brought on in the last minute for my second cap. We stayed at this hotel on a big hill, surrounded by sheep in the middle of the North Atlantic.

You wonder how your job has taken you to places like that. Same with some other trips, cities like Chisinău and Tbilisi in Eastern Europe.

Airport... hotel... pitch... stadium.

That's your itinerary. You might go for a half-hour walk on the morning of a game for couple of miles, but that's all you see. The flying can take its toll, but a win lifts everyone's spirits on the plane home.

The tournament experience was different... flying around France for Euro 2016 to play in Paris, Bordeaux, Lille and Lyon. Based in Versailles, we had downtime some afternoons. Myself and Ciaran Clark Googled *Things to do in Paris*... then ticked the list off one day.

The Champs-Élysées, Arc De Triomphe, the Eiffel Tower... we'd take photos of each other at these landmarks. Paris was full of Irish fans, so you're going to run into people. They were great though, no hassle and seemed surprised to see us out sightseeing. Boredom can easily set in on away trips. It depends on your personality.

Video games, darts, pool, cards... and I love watching TV series and films. I always had enough to keep me going.

Clarky was my usual roommate; we'd been friends a long time. If one of us wasn't in the squad, no one else came into the room to take that spot. That was the system. The Ireland management were clever in pairing people up.

Robbie Brady and Jeff Hendrick... the St Kevin's Boys' players.

Shane Long and Kevin Doyle... they'd the Reading connection.

Robbie Keane and Shay Given... the long-serving lads.

Seamus Coleman and James McCarthy... roommates since 2010.

On the bus, we'd start with Martin and Roy up top, then work our way through the team staff... with the players all further back. The more experience you have, you can push further to the back of the bus.

Robbie always sat on the back left of the bus.

He could demand that seat, he had the CV to back it up.

Callum Robinson came into the squad after Robbie left. A bubbly, lively character... and first day he sat in Robbie's seat. Jon Walters called him on it, just messing, but Callum smiled away, oblivious to it

My wife knew what it meant to me to be involved with Ireland. When I was still playing, I was lucky enough that Alanna was young so she didn't know any different. Of course, you'd miss them... an Ireland camp could mean eight to 11 days away from the family but we'd FaceTime often.

It was always nice to go see the Ireland lads.

We'd a tight-knit bunch around my age – Seamus, James McClean, myself, Clarky and James McCarthy. We were friends, there were no egos involved and that was reflected on the pitch.

IF I WON with Ireland, I came back to Hull on a high.

After the Wales game, I had my chest out. Seb Larsson was in the play-offs as well with Sweden. We watched the draw together... they got Italy, we got Denmark. He'd said before, that Denmark were one to avoid, a good team.

A month later we lose to Denmark... Sweden qualify after putting Italy out.

I come back to Hull and he's got his chest out; he's the one going to the World Cup. As much as managers might say it is great to see you play for your country, the focus quickly moves to Hull. The fans don't care about my experiences in Cardiff or Vienna.

Steve Bruce was asked once for his thoughts on me captaining Ireland?

He was in a press conference, and he'd been unaware of it. The Hull job was what consumed him. Steve never had a problem with you going, but he would go mad if you came back injured. Marco Silva used to message me the best of luck and tell me he'd be watching the games.

When I was with Reading, Paul Clement didn't want me to go to one Ireland trip. It was September 2018, when we got hammered 4-1 by Wales. He wanted extra training sessions as our results hadn't been great. The only way I wasn't going was if Martin didn't pick me.

He did, and then I had a massive argument with Clement about it. A sign that things wouldn't work out with Reading.

WHEN YOU JOIN a national squad, you wonder how the older stars will take to you? Meeting someone as iconic as Robbie Keane in Irish football was a big deal, but Robbie was always very good to me, I couldn't speak highly enough of him.

Even though Robbie was at the opposite stage of his career to me when we started, there was never a case that he was trying to keep his distance from the young lads that were starting out and trying to make their way in international football.

Joe O'Brien Whitmarsh was a young player with Cork City, who we had with the Ireland under-18s. He tore his cruciate early in 2022. I know too well how tough a setback that is to take as a player around that age, the uncertainty you face and the challenge to mentally come to terms with that.

Colin Brien as the Ireland coach wanted to do something for him and suggested to me that we try to get some video messages for Joe. So I messaged about 15 Irish senior players that I'd played with, wondering would they record themselves to send a few words to boost Joe's spirits.

First person back to reply with the video was Robbie.

Everyone got back to me within the next 12 hours with their clips, but Robbie was the first, straight back to me within 10 minutes.

He's probably the one person who could say he doesn't have to do it. Given his profile, I imagine he gets so many requests for stuff like.

But he does it anyway. Helps people out.

I've so much time for him.

I'm not sure Ireland will ever produce a striker like him again. Robbie had a street- footballer mentality. He thrived in tight spaces with his skill. Obsessed with goals, if it was a five-a-side in training, he'd run off and celebrate with a cartwheel if he scored. He prided himself on his finishing.

We played Gibraltar in 2014, the week before the Germany draw. Robbie got a hat-trick early on. He could smell blood in the water against teams. If a manager took him off when he was on two goals, there'd be uproar as he chased a hat-trick.

People said he scored loads of tap-ins but that was down to how good his positioning and awareness were. Some said a lot of his goals were penalties. But that showed how cool and calm he was under pressure.

I've wondered did Robbie really get the appreciation he deserved when he played... 68 goals is an unbelievable tally and that's enough proof of how incredible a striker he was.

IT WAS FRUSTRATING to hear during Martin O'Neill's time in charge that Ireland never played football the right way. Our midfielders were regularly in the spotlight for that. I was probably lucky that I didn't get as much criticism as Jeff Hendrick, Glenn Whelan or James McCarthy. My job was to win the ball back and get it to a better player.

Martin would always encourage us to pass; he'd have a go off me the whole time, saying he needed more. Fans and media want to see attractive football but results are the number one aim. It's a balancing act. Take the Slovakia game that Ireland lost on penalties in October 2020 in the Euro play-off. It might have been ugly, but Martin's teams would have found a way to win that game.

Some of the biggest and best moments you'll remember as an Irish fan were not games of beautiful football. But we still talk about them, how they made us feel emotionally. The Shane Long and Robbie Brady goals on teams I played on will be remembered as fondly as Ray Houghton in 1994 and Jason McAteer in 2001.

When those debates raged, I needed to learn to block out the noise.

I played one game for Ireland where I got a 5 out of 10 rating in a newspaper the next day. But in our camp afterwards, Martin and Roy were ecstatic about my performance. You have to step back and realise their views are most important.

It would bug me when suggestions were made that there was a lack of thorough analysis in the Ireland set-up. Martin looked back at Ireland games all the time; he'd be getting onto Ger Dunne, the lead analyst, for the footage straightaway if we lost, and for away games he'd watch them on the flight home. Same after training... the players headed for lunch and Martin to his office to watch videos of the session, see if he could spot anything.

The Ireland analysis team made three iPads available for the players. We used Hudl, the performance analysis app; everyone had a login and if you wanted to watch games or any opponent, there were specific clips available. We did collective team analysis but that extra individual stuff was up to each player.

I preferred to focus on myself, make sure I felt mentally right and fit, that my sleep and diet had been good. Seamus would watch wingers that he would be facing. Figure out their traits, like if they drop the shoulder to come inside. He found it very beneficial.

Defending set-pieces was at the core of Martin's philosophy.

We played Poland in November 2015, just after beating Germany. Their midfielder Grzegroz Krychowiak scored a goal after a corner came to him at the edge of the box and he fired it in through a crowd. That drove Martin insane.

We must have watched that goal back 50 times.

Same story with the Shaun Maloney goal for Scotland in 2014... lazy defending, someone not switched on and the team reacts too late.

Martin was adamant that games are won or lost with set-pieces. He went into them in so much detail, but the players were also involved in the planning. He would throw it out to the floor on areas like positioning... and who would be comfortable on the posts?

He took great pride in getting it right.

We had some great moments with Ireland, and supporters wanted that all the time. It's not that simple, however.

'It's easy to get to Manchester United. It's hard to stay there!' was a regular saying from Dwight Yorke at Sunderland.

That sums it up.

Consistency is what everyone in football is striving for.

12

Wanting the Whole World

AFTER THE FINAL whistle sounded at the Cardiff City Stadium in October 2017, one of the first people over to congratulate me was Seamus Coleman. I had captained Ireland to beat Wales 1-0 and keep our World Cup qualifying hopes alive.

The greatest night of my football life.

The importance of it was rooted in my personal long-term journey, but also my short-term one... recovering from the double knee surgery six months previously.

I was fortunate my injury hadn't kept me out for long, mindful of the struggles of others. In March, we drew 0-0 with Wales in Dublin... the game was overshadowed by Seamus breaking his leg.

Captaining my country in those 2017 qualifiers is my fondest football memory, but that only happened because Seamus got injured. After the final whistle, my main thought was for his well-being.

I visited him the next day in a Dublin hospital and after talking to him, I didn't worry about his ability to recover. With his strength of character, I was certain he would be back.

Two months beforehand, Hull played Chelsea and early in the first-half I came on for Ryan Mason. He had been treated after suffering a clash of heads. As he came off on a stretcher, I ran past and said, 'You'll be alright Mase!'

Later, myself, Tom Huddlestone and Michael Dawson went to the hospital.

It was a short 15-minute visit, it was horrible to see him like that. It was an awful accident which had such severe consequences. Ryan had fractured his skull and a year later was forced to retire from football on medical advice.

Witnessing two incidents like that on the pitch was unsettling.

You wonder… *Why them and not me?* I have a scar under my right eye from a game against Arsenal in 2015. Rose for a header with Laurent Koscielny and whatever way we landed, his boot hit me and slit my face. A couple of inches higher and I was in trouble. The Hull doctor said I was lucky I hadn't lost my eye.

It must have been frustrating for Seamus to watch that Wales game but his attitude after, in going around to everyone, summed him up.

It was a measure of the man.

Reaching the play-offs brought us one step closer to the World Cup finals… and I was desperate to qualify for Russia so that Seamus could play there.

THE PENNANT NEXT to my jersey was the giveaway.

I arrived into the dressing-room 90 minutes before kick-off against Moldova, on a Friday night in October 2017. The Irish kit lads had all our gear laid out as usual. When I saw the extra item next to mine, the realisation hit me.

I'm captain tonight.

Jon Walters had been deputising for Seamus, but he was out injured.

It was a stroke of genius not to let me know in advance. Instead, I had no time to become distracted about being Irish captain for a World Cup qualifier. Martin was good at that, in keeping everyone focused on the game. His tactic of delaying team announcements was criticised but it gave everybody a chance to stake a claim to start and helped keep players switched on.

I'd got back into the Ireland team in September against Serbia.

After drawing with Georgia, the midfield was changed with myself and Wes coming in. It was a game where the midfield area became a proper scrap. Nemanja Matić was a big powerful opponent but there is a mutual respect from that type of physical confrontation.

We lost 1-0… Aleksandar Kolarov scored a bullet.

So, in October we were very focused when facing Moldova. I was really glad for Daryl Murphy, he was clinical in scoring his two goals. We were there to win and once it was finished, all eyes turned to Wales.

IN THE FIRST-HALF in Cardiff, myself and James sandwiched Joe Allen in a challenge for the ball. It reflected our mentality… we had to win and would have run through him to do so. Joe was a brilliant link-man for Wales. But he had to go off; they were already without Gareth Bale, and then Aaron Ramsey had to drop deeper.

Their challenge was weakened.

I'd played against Ramsey many times for Hull against Arsenal. A nice, slick passer who you had to watch. I met his agent at the launch of the Fifa 20 video game; he also looks after James Maddison who we were doing some work with. His agent said Ramsey used to hate playing against me. He knew he'd get lumps kicked out of him.

There were times when Ramsey was miles ahead of me, and others when I frustrated the life out of him. There's a great photo of when we played Wales in Dublin. I won the ball back, Ramsey falls as he comes after me and he's pulling at my shorts to hold on. My attitude was to bring Ramsey to my level.

Though the best players don't come down!

The atmosphere in the stadium that night was highly charged with emotion. Wearing the armband sharpened my focus, but you couldn't help be taken in by the national anthems. The Welsh one was seriously impressive.

In the team huddle before, I kept reiterating that we would not lose the game. The winning goal was about Jeff Hendrick's control. No matter how many times I've watched it back, I'm still not sure how he didn't let the ball slip out of play. When he put in the cross, James McClean met it brilliantly with his right foot.

Near the end, I saw my name in lights as the ball bounced, just me against Wayne Hennessey racing from the Wales goal. *If I win it, I've got a tap in to an empty net in front of the Irish fans.*

But I'd nothing left in the tank, lunged in too late on Hennessey and got a yellow card. Martin O'Neill went mad at me privately after because I got suspended for the play-off first-leg.

After the game, I went back to Hull and came back down to earth, getting sent-off against Norwich. From the best feeling in the world, to a reminder about the day job.

But the Monday night memories of Cardiff will never fade.

JAMES MCCLEAN SIGNED for Sunderland in August 2011.

He was the same then as he is now – a nice, quiet fella, who's a bit dangerous when he has a phone in his hand. He likes a tight circle. His wife and children, his brothers and his parents; he holds them all close.

A good fella with a kind heart.

We got on well from the start. He's a month older than me but I was three years ahead of him in English football experience. At the start he was constantly going home to Derry but he settled well.

He's had a challenging time. In February 2021, he made the point that with the focus on racist discrimination against footballers, he had never got the same support when suffering abuse.

He mentioned former teammates not standing up for him. Privately, he clarified he wasn't taking aim at me, as I had helped him, but the reality was I could have done more. I distanced myself when he was subjected to horrendous stuff.

Why?

The simple truth was it was a world that I didn't want to get drawn into, potentially making myself and my family a target. My attitude was a bit selfish but I was fearful of getting involved.

I don't view James as a political person, more someone who is shaped by what he and his family have gone through. We've never really talked in depth about it but there are sensitive issues at play for them.

When at Wigan, he explained his decision not to wear the poppy. I felt it was reasonable and if people didn't agree with it, they could at least accept it.

He is the hardest working footballer I've met; fanatical about this fitness. When we lost to France in Euro 2016, the squad went out to drown our sorrows. James rarely drinks; he didn't that night and early the following morning he was in the hotel gym on a treadmill. He refuses to switch off.

Myself, Cally and Alanna were on holiday in Portugal one time, when we met James, his wife Erin and children as they were staying nearby. Later, Erin drove Cally back so they could get changed for dinner. I thought we'd relax by the pool, but James decided this was a chance to fit in a gym session… headed off and left me minding all the kids.

Before he scored the winner against Austria in November 2016, he got an epidural in his back. He wasn't supposed to play, could barely walk a couple days before, but was so determined. James and the doctor figured out how to get him through it.

He was the hero that night but he'd earned all the praise.

THE OTHER KEY man in Vienna was Wes Hoolahan.

When we started playing with Wes, we really got to appreciate the talent he possesses. He was the type of fella who would go training with a woolly hat, a big jacket, a pair of gloves and a pair of pants on. You never knew what mood he was in.

But in games, he could prove how gifted he was… running around, closing people down, that wasn't part of his game. He just wanted the ball and then he had the vision to pick off these stunning passes. I used to say to Wes… 'If you see me with the ball and I turn, I'm looking for you, no one else'.

It was a freezing night when we played Austria at the Ernst Happel Stadium. I was wrapped up in layers on the bench, when Glenn Whelan hurt his hamstring in the first-half. Suddenly, Martin is shouting and I'm running on without having warmed up. It took me a few minutes to adjust to the pace of the game and the conditions. But I grew into it, shielding the back four and in the second-half our confidence soared.

Kevin Wimmer tried to play the ball to David Alaba on the wing for Austria, when I went in to tackle. He felt he'd been fouled, but no whistle came and I played on. I was thinking of firing it down the line and, then I saw Wes out of the corner of my eye. Got the ball to him and he split the defence with this perfectly-weighted pass into the path of James, who shot to the net.

Players can be reluctant to admit it but the ball should always be given to the better player. I knew what Wes was capable of… my job was to supply him and that would help us win matches.

It is a real shame he didn't play more for Ireland. The breakthrough came too late in his career but he showed what he could do, as he still does at club level for Cambridge. A remarkable player.

TUESDAY NOVEMBER 14, 2017.

The Aviva Stadium is packed and full of anticipation. Three days before, we drew 0-0 with Denmark. I watch on in Copenhagen as I was suspended, but the lads put in a brilliant resolute performance. For the game in Dublin, I get back in the starting team… and I'm captain.

A place in the World Cup within our grasp.

And then at half-time, I'm done!

Martin calls out the changes.

Myself and Harry Arter are off.

Aiden and Wes in.

We're losing 2-1 after a perfect start with Shane Duffy's goal. I wished the lads around me well, got changed and back out to the stand to watch the second-half.

Denmark battered us 5-1. Christian Eriksen got a hat-trick, destroying our dreams of going to Russia.

Martin got it wrong at half-time.

If you want to take me off, that's fine.

Same with Harry. But don't take off your two holding midfielders. Get Wes or Aiden on for more creativity and then pin a player on Eriksen for the rest of the game. Instead, there was no protection for the defence and Eriksen has a field day.

My suggestion is different but I don't have Martin's experience. When he left Ireland, we chatted and went back over the years. He didn't apologise for that half-time decision but he did acknowledge that change could have been better.

We needed to hang in there at the start of the second-half.

Then throw the kitchen sink at it late on, if we were still losing 2-1. Think about the crowd roaring us on, willing the ball to go into the Danish net.

In September 2019, I was on radio co-commentary for *Off The Ball* as Ireland chased Switzerland. David McGoldrick equalised and that night I felt the energy in the stands pushing the team on.

Denmark could have been put under pressure, but they didn't need to worry as the goals were flying in. They started planning for Russia early.

I WAS IN a bullish mood before the game.

Seamus pulled me over an interview, where I'd said that Denmark didn't have the character and heart that we had. Seamus would have been more reserved… but I was declaring what I felt in my heart.

I had full belief in our team.

Watching the second-half was devastating. I wanted to get to the World Cup, not just for myself, but to give Seamus the chance to lead Ireland out. I was conscious I was a stand-in captain and always pointed out he was our leader. After what he'd been through with his leg break and people doubting him, imagine if he could have come back to that?

I felt powerless as that hope slipped away.

How long did it take me to come to terms with that night?

I'm still not sure I have.

The hurt lingers and I don't know will it ever completely go away. The end of my dream of playing at the World Cup.

We went up to the players' lounge in the stadium after. All my family were there. Cally had flown over... it was the first Ireland game she was at. Dad had been joking that she was never coming again after that result. He'd warned her that my mood wouldn't be great, but she knew that already.

All my buddies who I grew up with were at the game; they were going out in Dublin, I said we'd go meet them. Then Cally told me to go out and blow off some steam; she'd have an early night and head back to the hotel. It was really thoughtful of her.

I went out with the lads, drinking around Dublin. That group had been there for magical moments in my career but they also shared in the disappointments. They were gutted that we lost, but not as invested as I was.

'Ah look Dave, get over it... will ya?'

'Do you want a pint or what?'

That sort of talk pulls you back to reality. My last memory of the night is of the lads... one of them talking about his little boy growing up, and showing me photos.

It's a few hours after the biggest sporting heartbreak I've suffered. The pain of the loss and my performance is still raw, and I'm listening to how a toddler is growing.

And in a way it's nice, it gives me some perspective.

Life rolls on.

There is so much talk about winning and money in football, and not enough about teammates and lifelong friendships. I had the honour of captaining Ireland in the famous World Cup qualifier win over Wales in Cardiff in 2017 (above). Celebrating with James McClean and Robbie Brady.

Scrapping for Survival

WHEN YOU'RE IN a relegation scrap, you can't legislate for what other teams will do. Leicester City were bottom of the table at the start of April 2015 with just four wins all season in the Premier League to their name.

We were 15th and looked to be in a good position to survive.

Then Leicester won seven of their last nine games, going on this amazing run to push clear of the bottom three. The only match they lost in that time was 3-1 against Chelsea. They drew with Sunderland and won the rest.

They built a fortress at home to win five games.

Leicester caught everyone by surprise and didn't stop there. Twelve months on they won the title.

Hard to get your head around that.

We played a game less than them and only won twice in the same period. Those victories were in the space of four days… 2-0 away to Crystal Palace when Dame N'Doye scored twice, and 1-0 at home to Liverpool thanks to a Michael Dawson header. That burst of form at the end of April left us heading into May placed 15th in the table with four games left.

The one which cost us was the third last one, a 1-0 defeat to Burnley when Danny Ings scored. Our schedule that month was so tough. We had to play Arsenal, Spurs and Man United. All top five teams.

Burnley was the match to target for a win.

They were fighting for their lives as well.

After that game, we knew we were in trouble.

The team pulled together that year and we fought until the end. When the threat of relegation grows, you feel the tension around a club increase. Training gets more intense. People are a bit edgier in the dressing-room. You have to live with that pressure and can't crumble. My form was hit-and-miss that year.

Everyone had to look closely at themselves.

We needed to beat Man United on the last day, but Newcastle's win over West Ham took it out of our hands. We couldn't climb higher than 18th... only Burnley and QPR below us in the table at the end of the season. Looking around the stadium after the final whistle was a horrible feeling.

Everyone had taken a punch to the gut.

Life in the Premier League was over.

Back to the Championship and starting all over again.

Relegation has consequences. Players automatically lose between 40 percent and 50 percent of their wages. It's unsustainable to remain at Premier League rates, even if the parachute payments soften the landing a little.

There's cutbacks elsewhere in the club. As you get older you start to realise performances on the pitch will influence whether someone else keeps their job. Not just the manager and coaches, but the security team, the cleaners, the staff in the kitchen... all those people. If there are three laundry ladies working, that might be cut to two with relegation.

You've cost that lady her job.

I cared about that fact, others didn't.

It depends on the level you're invested in the club. A lot of lads kept their distance; all strictly business. At Hull I had more affection for the place, interacted with these people every day and that responsibility did get on top of me at times. My family got close to people at the club.

After I retired, I would still go to games and could have 20 or 30 people coming up to me to ask after dad, and my wife and my kids.

IT HAD BEEN a long season.

Despite losing the cup final, we still had the reward of European football as Arsenal had qualified for the Champions League. Instead of pre-season friendlies to feel our way back into action, we had Europa League qualifiers. I wasn't jaded, but didn't feel as fresh as I'd have liked.

We got past Trenčín from Slovakia in late-July... a 0-0 draw over there in a city called Žilina, and then won 2-1 back in Hull. We couldn't get past the play-off to reach the group stage though. Lokeren from Belgium beat us on the away goals rule. Robbie Brady scored twice in a 2-1 home win but we missed chances for the third. Another month on, and we'd have won but we just weren't at the proper pace of the game.

Pre-season is critical in getting yourself up to speed. Any injury at that time means you're playing catch up. I missed a lot of those in my career. In 2014, I hurt my back and it took until early December for my first league start of the season when we played Everton. That was the beginning of 14 starts in-a-row in the league. I had cemented my place again.

Frustration always sets in when you're not playing regularly.

The only time I accepted it was if the team was winning; you have to hold your hand up in that situation and respect what your teammates are doing.

We did decently in the cups that year... took Arsenal to a fifth round replay in the FA Cup, and reached the quarter-final of the League Cup before losing to Man City. In the previous round, I scored the last goal in a shootout to beat Leicester. I got subbed on in the 110th minute that night with penalties in mind.

I always enjoyed taking penalties... from underage days when dad would push me to take them to get on the scoresheet, to later assuming that responsibility for Hull. Penalties are an exercise in psychology. Placing the ball is important... don't have it elevated, set it properly. Have your mind blank.

Compose yourself. *Where am I hitting it?*

Always pick a side and never change your mind.

Wait for the referee's whistle... and STRIKE.

I didn't overthink them but started to practice more when I became Hull's regular taker in 2017-18. I'd get one of the young goalkeepers the day before in training, hit five penalties and he'd get £20 for everyone he saved.

That incentive ensured his focus.

WHEN RETURNING TO play any former club, there is an element of trying to prove a point. I had loved my time at Sunderland, only wishing I could have played more but for injuries. That Christmas in 2014 we headed to the Stadium of Light.

A rare good day with our first win in 10 games; we conceded after 30 seconds but bounced back for a 3-1 victory.

Heading back to an old ground like the Stadium of Light, there's some polite applause when your name is called out before and then you get pelters all game. I lived by the sword when I played Sunderland; had constant run-ins with Lee Cattermole. We were both experts at winding each other up. Though Bruce used to warn me before games not to get dragged into a personal battle.

One time we played them, and I bumped into Cattermole when out that night. He had a go off me on the stairs of a nightclub… wasn't happy with some of the challenges that day. Once I crossed the white line, I meant business, it was nothing personal. I enjoyed those contests with Cattermole.

Maybe he didn't expect it to get that heated. We'd got on well together at Sunderland, spent time together, like going for a round of golf. We were similar characters in our style of play. Whatever ill-feeling existed was gone soon enough.

EVERYONE WHO LINES out in the Premier League is a talented player.

Then there are levels which you discover as you play the best. I loved playing against the top six teams, to see these football icons up close. When I scored against Man United, Wayne Rooney hit this brilliant volley to draw the game.

Same when we beat Liverpool… Steven Gerrard tucked away a free-kick to level it.

These players can change games in a matter of seconds with a moment of magic. David Silva was a genius for Man City in midfield. You just couldn't get near him. He would speed the play up or slow it down when he wanted… take two, three touches to pass the ball… suddenly switch to one-touch passes.

You feel fine and think you have Silva pinned down.

Then he turns the heat up and the ball is flying around, or he makes a run and is gone out of reach. A game has accelerated out of your control. It's only when you're on the pitch playing against these players that you can understand that sense of powerlessness.

I scored against Silva once, when we were away to Man City in 2015. I gambled in following in an attack and after a Gastón Ramírez hit the post, I was there to fire in the rebound. It was great to go ahead, but then it was heartbreaking to see James Milner score a free-kick in the last minute to draw.

Still, a nice stat to complete the big three… Liverpool, Man United and Man City, and remember scoring against each of them in the league.

After we played Spain in 2013 with Ireland, we ended up on a night out in New York. I was in a bar and went to the toilets. A fella came stumbling through the door. We're next to each other at the urinals. I'm thinking this fella is full to the brim.

He says sorry. I notice the foreign accent and take another look at him.

'Alright David!'

Silva then recognises me.

'Heyyyyy… You always kicking me.'

'Yeah, that's because you're too good for me.'

We'd a good laugh at that.

IN THE SUMMER of 2015, the hangover from relegation lingered.

There was uncertainty, people got restless and the transfers rolled out. James Chester left for West Brom, and Nikica Jelavić left for West Ham. The Irish crew were gone… Robbie, Paul and Quinny all moving on.

Robbie got a route back to the Premier League with Norwich City… Paul and Quinny both went to Reading on free transfers. After a couple of years at the top, adjusting to the Championship was hard.

New faces came in… Sam Clucas, Moses Odubajo and Shaun Maloney played a lot. Everyone had to ask themselves the question… *Am I going to sulk or get promoted again?*

Amidst all that change, we turned it around. The lowest we were in the table that year was 7th; we were top in November, and again in February. The strong core of McGregor, Curtis, Huddlestone, Livermore, Dawson and Snodgrass remained. Abel Hernández was a goal-machine… he scored 22 that season. Andy Robertson nailed down the left-back spot, Harry Maguire came strong.

The start was positive.

The first three games set the tone with wins at home to Huddersfield Town and Fulham, and a draw away to Wolves. We went 11 games unbeaten for a time after September, really hitting our stride with five wins in-a-row around late October and early November. Five clean sheets as well in those games and 12 goals scored… I chipped in with a right-foot shot to round off a 3-0 victory over Ipswich Town and then scored the opener against Birmingham. City.

We should really have won the Championship but just hit a really bad patch around March, winning once in eight games. That knocked us back from the automatic spots. We were top of the table at the end of February, and down to fourth by April.

We pumped both Burnley and Middlesbrough 3-0 at the end of 2015, but they finished stronger to be in the top two.

In April, I was out with an injured hamstring and we were struggling. Steve Bruce called me into his office and asked would I play? I wasn't totally right but said I was good to go. I knew the risk and accepted it.

I captained the team in wins over Wolves and Reading, but that made my hamstring 10 times worse. The more I ran against Reading, the more I could feel it ripping.

Championship football can be a slog… 46 games in a season, not factoring in cup competitions. We had to go the extra mile with the play-offs. Midweek matches pile up… play Saturday, recover Sunday, light training Monday… play again Tuesday and start getting yourself right for the weekend again.

THERE WERE FOUR of us.

Hull, Brighton, Derby and Sheffield Wednesday in the play-offs and only one was going into the summer celebrating. Injury hit me at the worst time, I missed the last four games and the semi-final first-leg.

I watched in the stand as we beat Derby 3-0 at Pride Park.

We blew them away. Hernández with the opener, then an own goal, and Robertson scored the third in the 98th minute. The next few days I was fighting to get fit and came on at home for the second-leg.

Different story. Derby made a flying start and scored twice before half-time. I came on in the 52nd minute and we had to grind them down to go through.

Play-offs are mad games, there's this 100 miles an hour frenzy to them. The fans are all up for it, drama is guaranteed and previous form seems irrelevant. The final is termed the richest game in football… the prize of the Premier League means there's no escaping the importance.

Dad wasn't there… one of the few games he'd missed.

I didn't start; the timing of the injury was a killer and I couldn't get back into the team. I was not happy but had to accept it. After 30 minutes I got told to warm up. On four different occasions it looked like I was coming on for Diamé. Then, midway through the second-half, Diamé cracks one into the top corner. A wonder goal. Eventually I got on with five minutes to go. We won 1-0.

Afterwards I felt a bit detached from the celebrations, and it was hard to enjoy it properly. Maybe it's selfish, but I didn't feel I'd made a significant contribution. Part of my mood was due to the upcoming Euros and the worry Martin wouldn't pick me in the squad if I hadn't played recently for Hull.

That game was on a Saturday evening.

Later we went back to the team hotel for the party… Cally and my buddies were all there. I did really enjoy that night. We'd won at Wembley and I'd got to walk up those steps to get my hands on a trophy.

Next morning, I flew over to Cork to meet up with the Ireland squad for a friendly against Belarus.

It was a week of defining moments.

When a club gets relegated, everyone employed either at the Stadium of Light (above) or the MKM Stadium suffered. I was always fiercely aware of that responsibility, that it was not just about players, but the many hundreds of people whose careers can be in jeopardy once a club has to downsize.

THE FANS

FANS ARE THE lifeblood of football clubs.

I understood that straightaway in Sunderland and Hull. You play first-team in those areas and you're an important figure in their eyes. You will get stopped on the street. I'd always try to make time for people; catch me in a good mood and I could talk away for an hour.

Other situations were less ideal but you had to tolerate them. A Hull City fan in the park one day wanted a photo as I was trying to keep an eye on the kids running in the playground. He wasn't happy when I asked him to wait a few minutes, until Cally came to watch Alanna and Brody. But he did calm down; we took the photo and chatted away about Hull's form.

Hull is a big rugby league town so that competes for the sporting affections. Whereas, in Sunderland there was only one sporting show in town.

In recent years, the *Sunderland 'Til I Die* documentary on Netflix has given people an insight into the area; the level of passion amongst the fans had hit me years before. My red card against Porstmouth in February 2010 had caused a wave of abuse but then, a few weeks later, I was getting hailed for playing well against Man City.

I realised, in their eyes if you win you're right... and if you lose you're wrong. When you sign for a club like Sunderland, you have to buy into their way of thinking.

The fans work Monday to Friday to go and support Sunderland at the weekend.

That's what matters. It's almost Sunderland first and then your family, in that order. I loved that attitude.

I played at a positive time for Sunderland when they were in the Premier League, and I got on well with the fans because I wasn't a show-pony type player. I got stuck in and worked hard. That is the minimum standard the fans demand.

The documentary showed certain players didn't care about that.

Sunderland signed some wrong characters, and others threw in the towel. It is the definition of a big club with the scale of their fanbase and size of their stadium. It was heart-breaking to witness them slip down through divisions but Sunderland were always far too big for League One in terms of the fan numbers they attracted, the interest in their games. It just shows what happens when a club is mis-managed so much but it was great to see them climb back to the Championship.

I never had any hassle off Sunderland fans.

I lived within walking distance of the city centre. I'd stroll around shops like HMV to pick up a boxset, and you'd come across fans that way. When I joined first I was a complete unknown. Then when I started to play for the reserves, and we would get a few thousand at every one of our games, you'd be noticed. Once you break into the first team, there was more attention again. But I never had any bother or felt in a situation that I was better off not stepping outside the front door. It was more about filling time.

Sunderland fans are just so passionate. The result on a Saturday will make or break their mood for the week. As it is the only sporting show in town, football is ingrained in the culture of the place.

You could be doing a food shop... Asda, Morrison's, Tesco, didn't matter and people would be coming up to you, standing at your trolley and sometimes questioning what you were buying. They wanted to chat about the game the previous weekend and how were preparations going for the next weekend?

If it was pre-season the questions were fired at you.

'Who are the club signing?'

'How's the relationship between the manager and the players?'

'Are the injury problems going to clear up for the start of the season?'

They just care so much. It's not just a male-dominated thing either, Sunderland have so many local female fans that care just as deeply. Everyone in the community buys into it.

My parents came over once to Sunderland and we went all out for a dinner. A fella came over and sat down unannounced at our table to talk about a recent game and point out where I'd gone wrong in my performance.

People don't care if you think they're intruding.

I found it fascinating. It didn't overwhelm me. I'm a pure football fan, first and foremost. I never had a problem interacting with fans every day. A lot of players didn't live in Sunderland but I did.

When I joined I was a young kid who had come over from Cork, I was renting an apartment in the city around the corner from the stadium and that suited me. Everywhere you went, every single day you met fans. It was unavoidable.

....

HULL HAS A different sporting environment.

There are two rugby league clubs. Hull FC in the west and Hull KR (Kingston Rovers) in the east, and a cross-city rivalry takes place.

The football club is on its own, unifying the city. It is sort of isolated in a wider sense in East Yorkshire, with no major clubs nearby. Leeds are claimed by Hull fans as rivals. My first time playing against Leeds was in December 2012, while still on loan at Hull from Sunderland. I scored in a 2-0 in a home win, a nice positive note to finish the Christmas period and the year.

We played them a few more times in Championship games but Leeds have longer-standing rivalries with the likes of Manchester United. They see themselves as a bigger fish.

The fame thing, the business of being recognised is a strange one. There may be two rugby league teams here but definitely the footballers that I played with got recognised more. Hull is a unique place though. People don't really come up to you in the street. They'll know who you are, a player for their football club, but most people leave you alone.

I don't mind interacting with fans but I don't crave it. I've always found people here are just really nice and polite, not intrusive. Especially when I'm with my family, they don't hassle you. It's a nice environment.

You still get those experiences with fans even though I'm retired. I play five-a-side every week on a Wednesday night with a group of lads in their mid-twenties. A great bunch. One of them, when it was his girlfriend's birthday last year, invited me around to his place. I called over to the party for a few hours and this girl who was there started staring at me when I walked in. Turned out she was a big Hull City fan, had been going to games with her father since she was 10 years of age. She started talking to me about different games and players... she FaceTimed her dad and I was chatting away to him.

Another time last year, I just called into a local garage to get a new set of tyres for the car. The owner recognised me... a big Hull City fan, he got one of the other lads to sort me out, sat me down for a cup of coffee and we chatted away.

That sort of sums up the Hull fan experience. They're very genuine, very interested in the club and given the teams I was a part of, they just like taking trips down memory lane. It's really nice.

I've been living here 10 years and I've had a handful of bad altercations. One was when we were relegated the end of the 2016-17 season. I had a group of lads over from Cork for the game of the season when we played Tottenham at home. I was out injured at the time and we got hammered 7-1... Harry Kane scored a hat-trick. Our group decided to go out in Hull after the game, and ran into a few fans. Lads in their early twenties, they thought I was taking the piss that I was out after we got relegated.

I had another one night in a taxi queue, when I was waiting on my own, and group of four to five lads got stuck into me. Again, that was in the early hours of the morning, lads are full up on drink, so you leave it off.

Ninety-five percent of the time I've been here, people have been absolutely brilliant to me. They just love chatting and reminiscing about the big days, the trips to Wembley, the promotion challenges... the time in the Premier League.

....

AS A PLAYER, I generally tended not to go out at night too often in Hull. My thinking was if you're out on the town, it's very easy to bump into Hull fans. I tried to steer clear. Could go to Manchester if I fancied a night out... or when I was at Sunderland, I headed to Newcastle. Easier to slip under the radar. You meet people in those cities and you might get recognised but they don't care as you're not playing for their club.

In Hull, it was understandably different. The year we got to the FA Cup final, we played Brighton in the fifth round. Drew 1-1 down there, Yannick Sagbo scored late on for us. We had them back here for the replay a week later and beat them 2-1. It was a Monday night and we all went out after the win.

It's a different vibe during the week, a big uni night in Hull. There was around 16 of us who had headed out. Word got back to the club, and Brucey called a couple of the senior players the following day and he was going mad... he really went off on one.

'What the hell are ye doing going on a big night out in Hull?'

He wanted to know how many of us had there been.

'Sixteen out of the 20 in the squad.'

That stopped him. He realised that pretty much the whole lot had gone out. Everyone was in for the recovery training session the following day and getting ready for our game the next weekend. There was no splits in the group, so I think it reminded him we were pretty united and sticking together.

You just need to be careful and not slip into the trap of thinking you're untouchable. The status of a footballer changes things. There were times all my pals came over from Ireland and we headed out, walked into a restaurant and there's Steve Bruce with his wife. He's not stupid.

He sees six Irish lads all around a table with their best gear on, having some dinner, sinking a couple of pints and he's thinking where are we going after? It's not a case of having a bite to eat, head home and *good night.*

We don't look like a group having an early one.

....

THERE ARE SO many people working in the background in these football clubs who were good to me and I often think of them.

Steve Bruce used to make the point when the team was under pressure after a bad set of results and the prospect of relegation was looming large, that it wasn't us as players he was worried about, it was the staff around the place. He'd hammer that home to us. That motivated me to perform and the same went for the majority of our Hull squad in those first few years.

We had the right culture.

The club staff make these places special. If I go back to Hull games since I retired, the same security people are there to look after me and ask after my family. The same at Sunderland. They are the soul of a football club.

Joyce Rome is one of the nicest people I've ever met in my life, the club chef in Sunderland who was one of the breakout stars of the Netflix series. Viewers warmed to her; she was genuine in front of the cameras with the level of emotion she invested in the club. When I played for Sunderland she was exactly that way, hurting when we lost... so happy when we won. She's been there a long time, a mother figure to players.

If anyone needed anything food-wise, they got it; she would travel to all the away games on the team bus and look after us. A few years ago Sunderland played Hull and Joyce was still working for the club. I went onto the Sunderland bus after the game to say hello to her. A lovely woman.

They were always important to me... the people in the background at the club making the whole system work. I think of growing up in Cork, playing soccer for College Corinthians and our two main coaches, John Turner and Danny Drennan, who had sons playing. Their wives would take turns washing and ironing all of our kit. I didn't acknowledge it at the time but in later years I realised what John's wife Sally and Danny's wife Celine had done, how they were the example of the volunteerism that keeps sport going.

I learned that as well from my dad, how much unseen work he does for the hurling teams he has managed. I took that on and as I became a professional player I would consider all the other people who perform different roles that feed into the preparation of the team.

My interest in Sunderland will never wane, even though I'm not living in the area. Hull is my main focus given where I'm based but I still look out for Sunderland's results every week, just like I would those of Reading and Coventry.

The clubs that you play for have a huge role in shaping your football life.

Business as Usual

TWELVE DAYS AFTER Steve Bruce left as Hull City manager in 2016, we flew to Austria for a pre-season tour. The club was in chaos. Keith Bertschin, the first-team coach, turned up with his luggage only to be told he wasn't needed. Mohamed Diamé had just moved to Newcastle. Michael Dawson, Moses Odubajo, Allan McGregor, Alex Bruce and Harry Maguire all stayed home as they nursed injuries.

We had made no signings. Mick Phelan was caretaker manager. There were only 13 senior players on the plane with a group of under-23s.

We played a Turkish team in a friendly in Kufstein, a few miles from the German border... a beautiful place surrounded by snow-capped mountains. The day after a 3-1 win, a group of us took a cable car to the Asitz mountain station. Up there, 1,800m above sea level, with this stunning scenic backdrop, I suggested we take a photo.

Back row... Andy Robertson, Robert Snodgrass, Tom Huddlestone, Sam Clucas and Adama Diomande.

Front row... myself, Jake Livermore, Curtis Davies and Ahmed El Mohamady.

All the lads wearing the club gear.

Curtis put it on social media first with the caption... *Hull City squad photo 2016-17.* Then a few more did; it was a joke but we were making the point how small our squad was.

We'd that day off as we headed up to the mountains but were told not to go drinking. Livermore is an eccentric character, a superb teammate. Snodgrass is a born comedian, so quick-witted. The time the police phoned me over the Pardew head-butt, I suspected it was Snodgrass winding me up. The form was good amongst the lads.

There was a debate… *Would we have a drink?*

Snodgrass made a valid point.

If we all had one, how bad could the fallout be?

The club didn't have many players, they couldn't drop us all.

So, we started with a couple of pints and it turned into a day on the beer. We went tobogganing for a while, down a slide of a few hundred yards. Eventually we came down off the mountain, bumped into the physios and they could see we were all full up. Then Mick called a training session for 6pm.

He said we'd taken the piss going drinking.

We'd to do six runs between the penalty boxes… 20 seconds to go over and back.

We were all moaning… Snodgrass was cracking jokes but we just got through it.

Then, every first-team player beat the youngsters in the running. Mick went absolutely berserk at them… he made all those lads do another six runs.

NIGHTS OUT WERE a staple part of pre-season tours. If there was an unplanned one when Steve Bruce was in charge, he got over it if the whole team was together. If the group splintered into twos and threes, there was a problem.

On one trip to Portugal, he ordered us to stay in. By the end of the week, we were getting restless. Dawson organised a bus to come collect us. We'd a 22-man squad; two lads were Muslims who don't drink.

The bus Dawson ordered had 19 seats. I volunteered to make my own way in, went to the hotel reception and ordered a taxi. Turned away and walked straight into Steve Bruce, Steve Agnew, Steve Clemence and Gary Walsh.

'Where are you going?' asked Agnew.

'Nowhere!'

'Come on, don't forget we all played,' said Clemence.

Bruce looked at me. 'How many of ye are going?'

'Twenty!'

'Okay, make sure everyone's home at a reasonable time… and ye don't leave anyone behind. Go and enjoy yourself!' Couldn't argue with that.

I headed in to meet the lads, walked into a bar and told them the gaffer had given us the green light. A massive cheer went up.

Leonid Slutsky also took us to Portugal.

Dawson was captain and I was vice-captain. We figured one of us needed to get permission for the night out, so I went to Slutsky. There was no problem, but he put a cap on it of five drinks.

That was never going to be adhered to.

We'd a bus to the airport the next morning.

Dawson is an early bird, so myself and Allan McGregor stayed near him and gave him room keys. Told him not to forget to wake us. Greggsy was brilliant fun on a night out… a Rangers man, but I got on so well with him. We got back around 6am, and Dawson came in a couple hours later and chucked buckets of water over the two of us to wake us up.

We were pushing time, but we'd packed the night before and made the bus. A goalkeeper, Jon McLaughlin had come on trial; he'd done really well but kept the bus waiting that morning. When we got back to England, he was never seen in Hull again.

WHEN WE GOT back from Austria before the 2016-17 season, there was still mayhem at the club. The players were united. We finally made some new signings, like Ryan Mason, Markus Henriksen and David Marshall. From the outset we were written off as relegation favourites.

Then we made this amazing start. Played the champions Leicester City in the opening game of the new Premier League season, and beat them 2-1.

Won 2-0 away to Swansea, scoring twice in the last 11 minutes. Lost to Man United, but only after a 92nd minute Marcus Rashford goal. Then grabbed a draw with Burnley, when Snodgrass scored in the 95th minute.

Our fight and spirit dragged us through. Mick Phelan had us so well drilled and organised. You always believe you can sustain that momentum, but it's a fairytale.

We didn't have enough first-team players.

Reality started to intrude.

We only won once in the next 18 games, right up until the middle of January. If we had strengthened the squad a bit more it would have helped, but the depth wasn't there. It goes back to Steve Bruce's exit the previous summer... he knew what was coming.

We suffered some bad defeats.

Arsenal 4-1.

Liverpool 5-1.

Bournemouth 6-1.

That last one was a real concern; losing to the big teams is one thing but a thrashing like that makes everyone – manager, players, owner – start to question things. There was a personal consolation in the Liverpool game, scoring a goal at Anfield. It was my last one in the Premier League. Snodgrass swung in a corner, it broke and I caught it cleanly to lash in a shot. A rare cause for cheer that day.

We were down to 10 men after half an hour. I was brought on to play right-back after Elmo got sent-off. It's the worst feeling as a footballer, coming on when your team is getting pumped. Subs are meant to make an impact but when everything is in disarray, you're not going to turn it around.

When I scored, we were down 3-1 but I didn't celebrate, just sprinted back to our half. Roy recalled the incident later at an Ireland camp.

'Why did you run back so quickly?'

I pointed out that's what teams do in that situation; they try to get the game going again in the hope of a comeback.

'Yeah, but ye were 3-1 down, ye weren't getting back into that game. You might as well have taken your time and enjoyed it.'

He had a point.

Liverpool ripped us apart that day. In the second-half, the ball went out for a throw. The home fans were heckling me as I went to take it.

'Come on man, hurry up!'

'We're 4-1 down and have 10 men! I'm not rushing for anyone.' A big group of the crowd actually start laughing.

After that game, myself, Jordan, Adam Lallana and James Milner were all due to go out. Our wives had arranged it; we were all going to Manchester for dinner. I'd got to know the lads through Jordan, we'd often meet up. I'd always tell Cally... Don't plan anything after games, the result would dictate my mood.

If I've played and we've got a result, then let's do whatever you want afterwards.
This night was long arranged.

Cally's mother was looking after Alanna and we'd booked a hotel. Then Hull got hammered. The only reason I went out was that scoring the goal at least helped me. The Liverpool lads only went out because they had got a good result. When we'd beaten them 3-1 in 2013, there'd been plans to meet after but that got binned once they lost, as Jordan was raging.

Football is a small world that sparks plenty of relationships.

I'm very good friends with Seamus Coleman and with Jordan Henderson. One's the Everton captain, the other's the Liverpool captain. They hated one another for years. Openly hammered each other when talking to me. I used to laugh and tell them they were both so similar. Their drive and desire, their family values… their no-nonsense attitude to drinking!

When Seamus broke his leg in the Wales game, there was a Merseyside derby soon after. Jordan wrote a piece on him in the match programme. Wished Seamus well… with such a massive rivalry, you want the best players involved in derbies and it was a shame Everton had lost their captain.

Seamus rang me after.

'Your mate is actually alright.'

I rang Jordan later to tell him and now I would say, they're not friends… but there's a mutual respect there. It's funny how it evolved over time.

WE WERE FORTUNATE that Mick Phelan took over as caretaker, someone we knew. The strange thing was why it took him so long to get the Hull job full-time? He was eventually appointed in October but the results piled the pressure on and by January he was gone.

After four years of Steve Bruce, we saw a lot of change. In my last two years at the club, I had four managers… Mick, Marco Silva, Leonid Slutsky and Nigel Adkins.

Marco was a leftfield appointment. He'd managed in Portugal and Greece. Paul Merson famously wasn't too impressed on *Soccer Saturday* on Sky Sports. 'Why's it always got to be a foreign manager?'

I'd a more open mind. He was my new manager and I'd to get on board. It wasn't like I had 10 clubs knocking on the door looking to take me.

Marco changed the philosophy and freshened it up. If we had Marco from the start of that season, we would have stayed up. The first day he took over, we trained for three hours. I've never trained so long for one session in my life. Everyone was blown away by the attention to detail. It wasn't hard, but Marco walked us through everything he wanted from us.

Did that every day for weeks.

The tough thing for Marco was, in 2017 it felt there was a constant flow of big names exiting Hull. It started with Snodgrass and Livermore moving in January. Five players joined, but all on loan, and building cohesion wasn't easy. By the end of May, Marco himself had departed. Then Harry, Andy, Tom, Elmo and Curtis all left over the course of June and July.

It felt surreal.

I was looking around wondering... *who's staying?*

When I moved in 2018, someone mentioned it was time to turn off the lights on my way out. A sledgehammer had been taken to the squad that had won promotions and reached the FA Cup final.

There was nothing left.

WHEN LEONID SLUTSKY took charge, that lack of togetherness was the same problem. We played Derby.

Fikayo Tomori had joined on loan from Chelsea.

The first time I met him properly was in the tunnel before the game.

How can you strike up a relationship like that?

All these loan moves didn't help. When we had days off, those boys were from London and went home to see their families. Of course, I'd no problem with that but we couldn't build a culture in the club. The first time I'd signed for Hull, everyone lived in the general area. When you sign for a club, you need to buy into it and the area where the fanbase are from.

I did that and felt more at home as a result.

WE PLAYED MAN United three times in early 2017.

Lost the first-leg of the League Cup semi-final 2-0, won the second-leg 2-1 and then drew 0-0 in the league. I started right-back in all three games.

There was a good buzz to those cup semi-finals on January midweek nights.

We pushed them all the way in the second-leg. Huddlestone opened the scoring, Pogba equalised and then I crossed for Oumar Niasse to score with five minutes left. That was the only time I beat United in my career, albeit we lost on aggregate and missed out on Wembley so it felt a hollow success.

Myself, Harry Maguire and Sam Clucas were talking before that trio of Man United games. We all wanted the same shirts… Pogba, Rooney and Zlatan.

So, we made a pact… and rotated through the fixtures so we could get them all. Plenty of players don't care about swapping shirts. I like to get them as mementos and a reminder of happy times.

In the second-leg, United get a corner near the end… Zlatan is walking backwards, I'm minding the front post.

He stands on my foot and turns.

'Woah, sorry big man!' he says.

'You're a bit bigger than me!' I tell him.

He just laughed and after the game I asked for his shirt.

'No problem my friend… I'll give it to you inside.'

So, we go into the tunnel and swap. I always kept a Sharpie marker in my washbag. The shirts are great… if you can get them signed they're even better. Later I walked out and Zlatan was leaving at the same time. He's this iconic figure who has played for Ajax, Juventus, Inter, Barcelona, AC Milan and PSG.

It's unlikely we'll cross paths again.

One chance.

You don't get anything if you don't ask.

'Zlatan! Have you got a second to sign the shirt?'

'No problem, my friend. Can you sign your shirt?'

'Yes Zlatan… absolutely I can!'

I have that shirt framed and hanging on the wall in my house. I haven't yet seen 'Meyler 7' in the Zlatan Hall of Fame. I liked his larger-than-life persona, as he backed it up on the pitch and I found him just really respectful that time.

Some don't approve of swapping. Roy hates it.

What probably frustrated him more was people asking him for his shirt. Jordan has never asked anyone for a shirt in his life. Seamus would only swap if he's playing against Ireland lads. But it doesn't bother me. I grew up a football fan and I'm still one… the memorabilia is cool.

I always did it off the pitch, away from cameras and the eyes of the world. You think of the criticism when André Santos got Robin Van Persie's shirt in 2012 in front of the whole stadium.

Got to be smart, don't give people a chance to slate you.

I've a nice collection. Under Trapattoni, Ireland played Spain at Yankee Stadium in New York in 2013. The final whistle was about to blow as I asked Cesc Fàbregas for his shirt.

Then he wanted mine.

It was the alternate black jersey that had been brought out. He collected shirts from every country he played against and hadn't got an Ireland one after Euro 2012.

MARCO SILVA ALMOST engineered the great escape.

Seventeen points from his first 11 games, but we only got four from his last seven. Finished the season getting walloped 7-1 by Spurs, as Harry Kane scored that hat-trick. That game was on a Sunday, Marco resigned on the Thursday and by the Saturday he was as the new Watford manager.

That's football, it's a mad business.

That year was my last taste of the Premier League. I'd reached the point of no return and anyway I was distracted. The struggles with my knees had returned.

In April, we were at the end of a training session, when I went through one-on-one. David Marshall came flying out from goal and collided with my knee. I heard a click in my left knee.

It was the right I had damaged twice before, but waiting for the physio to come over felt like an eternity. He instantly said my medial was gone. I told him to check my cruciate, so he performed the test.

Lying on the pitch, I'm thinking if this is my third cruciate... *I am done. Game over.*

It wasn't. I still needed a scan to confirm it but the signs were good. The diagnosis was a Grade 4 MCL tear, which is still horrible and required another operation. The surgeon felt this was a good time to clean up my other knee as well. I wish I hadn't got that second knee surgery done, it didn't help me in the long run.

The physio Rob Price and the doctor Mark Waller at Hull, two people I respect, felt it was best for me at the time. I don't blame them, I'd always have taken their advice.

The club sent me down to a specialist in London to get it done. Every surgery I've had, I've wanted to start the journey back on my own. Didn't want people at my bedside. When I woke after that surgery, I was high on the pain medication and not sure what I was raving about.

Next thing the door opened… and Cally was there.

Hull gave me two options for the trip home – get the train or they'd send a car down. I wasn't sitting in a car from London to Hull. I preferred the train, felt I could get up to move if I needed, but the journey was still a disaster.

Reaching Platform 6 at King's Cross Station usually requires a few minutes' walk from the entrance. It took me an hour and 15 minutes on crutches. Cally was in tears. I nearly passed out three times, sweating and exhausted.

She bought Lucozade to give me an energy boost. Got on the train eventually and sat at an angle, flopping my leg up on the table.

For the first three weeks at home, I slept on the couch. Didn't have the strength to go upstairs; needed help to go to the toilet and to shower.

One night, I'm lying in the living room and needed to go to the toilet. Wanted to do it myself… took me 45 minutes to muster the energy to lift my legs off the couch, the sweat pouring off me. I'd accepted at one stage I was going to have to p*** myself. Then one of my crutches fell and made a loud bang.

Cally is a light sleeper and she ran downstairs worried. I told her I was just trying to get to the bathroom. She broke down at that sight… my inability to stand up and hobble over a few yards.

I was stubborn, clinging to my independence.

We weren't going out when I had twice done my cruciate. Seeing me in this helpless state with my knees in bits, that was a proper eye-opener for Cally. A severe injury will generate bad days. You have to accept them, when the pain in your knee can flood your mind with negative thoughts.

Just have to ride them out.

I retired at the age of 30 and they still crop up, the mornings when you wake up… feel that knee pain and know it'll bother me during the day.

To see me like that in 2017 was hard for Cally.

We both have traditional values. Husband and father is the alpha male character. There I was at my weakest and most vulnerable. When tearing my cruciates, I was young and fearless, and could focus on myself. Now there were others to consider. Cally had to deal with a 28-year-old limping about… and look after our 15-month-old daughter Alanna.

It'd be a shock to anyone's system.

The knee injury did cause me to relocate to the Portuguese sun that summer. Six weeks in the Algarve. I first booked a family break for a fortnight and then Hull wanted me to extend it because one of the physios was out there on holidays. So, I'd work with him at 10am while our wives, who are really good friends, went off to the beach. After that, Hull were coming out for pre-season, so they just told me to stay on. Cally loved it, she didn't go home.

For those first few weeks, I was stuck in a dark tunnel with no flickers of light appearing. But you just keep going. There is no choice and gradually it improves.

Then six months after needing guidance to get to the toilet, I captained Ireland to beat Wales in Cardiff.

Jordan Henderson (top) and Seamus Coleman are two of my best friends, but as rival Everton and Liverpool captains (and England and Ireland internationals), they had zero time for one another for years. I helped them change that outlook... a little!

CALLY

I MET CALLY when I was 25. The best thing that ever happened to me.

She helped slow me down and mature. Alex Bruce introduced us. I was one of the few Hull lads who was single. Alex and Cally had a mutual friend, and he set us up. I got her number, started messaging, and the rest is history.

When we started going out, she lived in Manchester and I was in Hull.

We were back and forth all the time. I put down the marker about football early on. For our third date, we went to see Liverpool play an FA Cup fourth round replay. A Wednesday night in Bolton... very romantic setting.

Cally only lived about 40 minutes from the ground. I was going to see Jordan play, so picked her up, we went for dinner before and then to the game.

Cally's family are all Man City supporters, old school fans from the Maine Road days. Her grandmother has an unbelievable match programme collection. Her mum is from the city, her dad is Scottish but he's settled in Manchester a long time. Cally's football knowledge has got better over the years.

She knows how much I'm into it and takes interest. If there's a big Champions League match on, we'll watch it together.

When our kids arrived, it grounded me. Alanna was born in January 2016, Brody in April 2019. After Cally first became pregnant, the goalposts were shifted. She made me realise that my life couldn't be training, matches and nights out.

Cally would have worked in her family's clothing supply business, but she moved down before Alanna was born, to Cottingham, where I had bought my first house outside Hull. We're still there, well settled.

We got married on February 15, 2018.

We'd initially planned a big wedding but decided to postpone it as Cally was pregnant, and then she sadly had a miscarriage.

We were going to New York, just the two of us later in 2017, and I tried to arrange another wedding over there. I'd seen Shane Lowry got married over there... had met him a few times, he's just a massive Irish sports fan.

So, I spoke to Shane about where they went, the photographer they booked and everything like that. But then Cally wasn't as big a fan of a New York wedding with no family present. It dragged on, until we were arguing over the date one night and then she just booked a registry office in Beverley near us.

We set a date, our families came over... and we got married.

I trained that Thursday morning with Hull as we were away to Chelsea in the FA Cup on the Saturday. Then the game was changed to Friday night because of TV coverage. I explained the whole situation to Nigel Adkins and he was brilliant. He told me... get married, stay for few hours for dinner and get the last train down to London.

After training, the rest of the players were getting ready to go to the train station. Frazier Campbell asked me for a lift to the hotel where we were meeting first.

'I can't.'

'Why?'

'I've got something on.'

'What could you have on?'

'I'm actually getting married.'

He started laughing, he couldn't believe it. I'd kept it quiet, just didn't want to jinx it after the other postponements... and Frazier started telling the other lads. It was a strange experience in a way, particularly the train journey that night, but still special and we'd a great time.

I want to do something when we're married five years. A big party to mark it with all our family and friends. Cally isn't religious but my dad is and I would like to get a Catholic blessing.

I started in the game at Stamford Bridge. We lost 4-0, conceding all the goals in the first-half... and I missed a penalty in the second-half.

A couple of days I'll never forget.

AS A FAMILY, the year 2017 tested us in ways we could have never imagined. Cally had three miscarriages.

Devastating moments.

One happened the day Ireland played Wales in March.

Cally rang, traumatised by the experience. There were ambulances outside my house in Hull and I was in a hotel room in Dublin preparing for a match. Martin O'Neill and dad both said to go be with my family. The next flight was a few hours later to Manchester and it would take another couple of hours to get to Hull.

Cally's family had arrived to look after her. I weighed everything up, decided to play the game and head home the next day.

In September 2019, I did a radio interview with Joe Molloy on the *Off The Ball* sports programme on Newstalk, a station in Ireland. I shared my story of that time. He pointed out that fans could have hammered my performance, not realising the trauma of that day. No one really knows what's going on behind it all with a player.

For the first two miscarriages, I focused on supporting Cally, but the third hit me the hardest. I thought I wasn't going to have another child and I was desperate for Alanna to have a sibling.

I didn't know how to cope. Bad moods.

Drinking at home. It was around then I was back in Cork and had that video recorded of me drunk, which was later uploaded to Facebook. I lost my way. I didn't confide in anyone and soon hit rock bottom.

The Hull physio Alan Peacham asked Brian Lenihan one day was I alright? Brian had sensed I wasn't. The club doctor Mark Waller called me in and I told him everything. They set me up to speak to someone. That process was hard. It helped a little but I sort of resolved it myself, found a way to get going again. Something as simple as getting out of bed early on a day off, and planning something to do.

Brian is five years younger than me. Another Cork lad who started off at Corinthians and later signed for Hull. He made his first-team debut in April 2016. I was in Paris that weekend but Steve Bruce gave me the heads up, so I arranged for Brian's family to be flown over to see Hull's game.

Brian used to come around to our house all the time. Cally would cook dinner or we'd play some pool.

A great fella.

MYSELF AND CALLY have two great children. We feel very fortunate after everything we've been through.

When Alanna arrived, it was a shock to the system like it is with any first child. Cally's mum was a huge help; I probably should have done more. After Brody was born, I was aware and involved from the start.

My daughter knows that daddy played football, but Brody is too young. I retired seven months after he was born. It's a shame I couldn't go on longer so he could have some recollection of me playing. But you can't have it all your own way.

I was retired about six months when Covid brought the whole world to a halt and we were locked down. My dad thought it would be a great time for me to stand still and reflect. I found it very difficult though, going from getting up every day to go training to... suddenly, not being allowed leave my house. Don't get me wrong, everyone struggled during the pandemic and many people suffered far more serious problems than I did. That was a really tough time for a lot of people. I was fortunate that I had retired from a job which had paid me well and I'd been able to put away a few quid. I didn't have the hardships others faced in losing jobs and incomes, or the serious situations that frontline workers had to deal with.

I'm fully aware of putting my challenges into proper context.

It was still a frustrating time as I was adjusting to retirement and wanted to go headlong into the world of coaching. I had to be patient and wait for that time to pick back up. It was lost time, but I'm sure everyone looks back on those months in 2020 and '21 in a similar way.

The flipside was it was great getting so much time to spend with my kids after years of being focused on training and travel involved with football. That required a change for Cally; she obviously wasn't used to me being home 24-7. It was a strain on our relationship for those first few weeks, everyone stuck at home together, but we figured it out and all got a routine that worked for us all.

Being home more often turned out to be the best thing that happened to me as a father, spending so much quality time with my kids. As tough as the lockdowns were in so many ways, it brought us closer together as a family.

Removing my Stripes

IN THE SUMMER of 2018, I left Hull City.

It was March when I found out the end was in sight. At breakfast before training, the Hull press officer Luke Cash came up to me.

'Dave, I'm sorry... the club aren't extending your contract.'

'What do you mean?'

'Oh s**t, do you not know?'

'No.'

I was confused. Later, the club would make their contract offer with a substantial 40 percent cut. I knew they were trying to get wages under control. The first year we got promoted with Hull, the average player wage was £10-12,000 per week. The second time we got promoted it had gone up to £25-30,000.

Finances were a tricky thing to navigate.

I played 191 times for Hull and if I hit the 200-mark, I got a bonus. It was notable at the end of my last season, I didn't play much. I understood decisions had to be made but I deserved more respect and to be told in a decent and formal way, not to discover through the media officer that I was heading for the exit.

AT THE HULL Player of the Year awards, the lads would all go to the director's box beforehand to meet the club owners, the Allem family. Ehab Allem was heavily involved but his father Assem had started everything and he and I met that night at the end of the season.

'David, I've heard that you're leaving!' said Assem.

'You need to come see me… we can sort this out.'

It was an awkward moment with someone I'd so much time for. Assem didn't seem to know what was going on. I didn't end up chasing him for that conversation… in my mind I was gone.

Aseem was born in Egypt and famously came to England in the 60s with £20 in his back pocket. Joined a company, Tempest Diesels, worked his way up and then bought it… renaming it Allam Marine. They manufacture generators.

He lives 15 minutes away from me now, a multi-millionaire in a modest sized house. Assem took over as Hull City chairman in 2010. He's done so much good for the club that all the recent upheaval is sad. Plans to change the name to Hull Tigers, to further develop the club's image, caused so much anger amongst fans.

I played in the most successful Hull team of all time and have fond memories of the place. But they had so much player and managerial turnover, that we lost stability.

The Russian coach Leonid Slutsky took over from Marco Silva in June 2017, lasted six months and then Nigel Adkins came in. Nigel was my last manager at Hull. The most positive man I've ever met in my life. Every morning he'd bounce into the training ground. You'd wonder did he ever have an off day.

Hull were far from promotion that season… we finished 18th.

I played my last game in April, a 2-0 defeat to Cardiff City. It was good of Nigel to play me, the last home game of the season is a traditional farewell to the fans. I got to walk around after to say goodbye and had Alanna with me.

It was sad. After six seasons and plenty of highs… but the end had come.

PLAYERS RARELY LEAVE a club without another offer. After the revelation in March, my agent Neil Fewings got to work. Steven Gerrard wanted to sign me for Rangers. I turned that down… would have caused too much hassle with the Ireland connection.

There was talk of Nottingham Forest, and I nearly signed for Leeds but the money wasn't good enough.

Reading looked like the best option.

Their manager Paul Clement flew to Dublin to meet me in June, when I was studying for my B coaching license. We chatted for an hour over coffee, and I was impressed by him and excited by the challenge.

The four-year contract offer was a good deal at the age of 29. But the medical raised concerns over my knee and the offer was cut to two years, with a possible option of another year. I resented that change while also understanding it. Reading had to rely on proper advice.

WHEN JOINING SUNDERLAND and Hull, I just had to pack my bags and go. Signing for Reading, I had more to consider with a wife, a daughter and another child on the way. Cally was settled in Hull but there's no time to debate, you have to leave.

They moved to Reading after pre-season and we rented a house. Thankfully, we didn't buy and kept our place in Hull.

Maybe that was a sign we didn't commit fully to the change. It was a four-hour drive for Cally's family from Manchester, more convenient for mine as we were close to Heathrow Airport.

Dad would fly over every Saturday; Alanna waiting with her toy bricks to build towers with grandad.

Do I regret moving to Reading?

Not a bit.

Cally had three miscarriages before our son Brody was born in April 2019. Being in Reading allowed us access to a specialist nearby in London and he resolved a blood clotting problem that she had.

The football side to our Reading story was difficult, but the move helped our family in the most important way.

PAUL McSHANE AND John O'Shea were familiar faces when I joined Reading. Paul was there a while and warned me there were a few bad eggs in the squad. Straightaway, I realised the problems with the club's culture… the time players showed up, how they trained, their demeanour.

That stuff needs to be rooted out because it can ruin a team.

The season began against Derby; Frank Lampard's first league game in charge of them. We took the lead in the second-half but Mason Mount equalised and then Tom Lawrence scored an injury-time winner. A week of sporting heartbreak.

The previous Sunday, dad was manager when Cork lost an extra-time epic to Limerick in the All-Ireland hurling semi-final.

I'd flown back after the game in Croke Park... still devastated for him.

Results didn't improve for Reading. No wins in our first six games left us second from bottom. On September 1, 2018, I started at home against Sheffield Wednesday and got taken off after an hour. That was the end of my Reading career.

I never played for the club again after that Saturday afternoon.

I got slaughtered by Reading fans for my displays, starting with the Derby match. Early defeats soured the mood at the club, and their frustration grew as the season progressed and Reading finished 20th, just clear of relegation.

I tried my best to break into the squad, and had plenty of conversations with Paul Clement, but got nowhere. I'd fallen out of favour, and experiencing that rejection was all new to me

There were two away games in November against Wigan and Leeds. Clement wanted me to travel as we were staying up north for a few days.

I was desperate to get back on the bench and figured I would when he brought me on that trip.

I didn't make the squad for either game. Clement wanted me around to help raise the spirits but I wasn't there to be an entertainer.

Hard times like that cause you to fall out of love with the game. It's never been about the money for me. It's great to earn a salary at that level and it has set me up for life, but I wanted to play. People said at least I was getting paid at Reading, but I shouldn't have been because my job is to play football and I wasn't doing that.

You try not to take it home with you, but I imagine for Cally I was a nightmare to live with. At the club to make up the numbers... soul-destroying. I always wonder what I could have done differently but the whole move was just a disaster from the start.

In early December, Clement was sacked and before Christmas the new boss arrived.

José Gomes from Portugal.

ON HIS FIRST day, Gomes asked to see me.

Eight players were brought in one by one. All told we could leave. Gomes apologised but said he had too many players.

Happy Christmas.

Now, there's the door!

I wondered were the shots being called above the manager. I left the room that day in a blur of emotion. Then I saw the kitman packing up my locker.

I couldn't change with the first-team anymore, train or eat with them… or speak to the manager again. I'd never had problems with any club I'd been at before… this was a bleak end to 2018.

Managers came and went during my final seasons with Hull, including (from left) Marco Silva, Leonid Slutsky and Nigel Adkins, who was the final boss I worked with for the Tigers. On the lookout for a new club, I was told that former Liverpool legend Steven Gerrard wanted me to join him at Rangers, but that move would never have worked out for me.

BOLO, SHANE AND CO

ONE OF THE most interesting players that I was fortunate to get to line out with was Bolo Zenden at Sunderland. What a player and what a career he'd had. By the time our paths crossed he was in the final stage as a player but he had packed in so much before that. Starting off with PSV Eindhoven, then a move to Barcelona for a few years. Went to England and played for Chelsea, Liverpool and Middlesbrough. Bit of time in France with Marseille. Won the Eredevisie and La Liga, a few Cup competitions in England. Played for The Netherlands in the 1998 World Cup and Euro 2000.

He was also on the pitch for one of the most famous days in Irish football history when we beat them 1-0 in September 2001 in a World Cup qualifier in Dublin.

I'm a football fan at my core, I used to love to pick the brain of a player like that. Think of all the great players he had encountered and had as teammates. Tell me your stories.

IN JANUARY 2020, HULL played Chelsea in the FA Cup and I got asked to do punditry in the studio for BT Sport. Went in and sat down in this portakabin beforehand... I was next to Joe Cole, Steve McManaman and Glenn Hoddle.

Glenn was talking to me about my career, going over games he'd watched and picking my brain on various things. An incredible fella. I'd so much time for him because he was so nice to me. Then, when time came for him to go and get make up done before the TV started, I was sitting down next to McManaman.

I'll just never forget how he was with me. I mean if you're sitting down with Steve McManaman, you're going to want to talk to him about Real Madrid. He was there for the Galactico years and I was far from the first to be pressing him as to what they were all like – Figo, Zidane, Raul, Ronaldo, Roberto Carlos, Casillas, Hierro.

McManaman talked away about what they were like in training, their skill levels, their characters. It was an amazing list of world-class players to have as teammates. The fact that he fitted into a squad like that showed how good a player he was.

I met Jonathan Woodgate on a night out once, a lovely fella, and I remember picking his brain on his Real Madrid experience. When Tom Huddlestone signed for Hull, I got something out of that. He was only three years older than me but I wanted to get all his memories about playing for Tottenham in the Champions League... like that game against Inter in the San Siro.

It was an amazing match, they lost 4-3 but had been down four goals at half-time and Bale got a hat-trick in the second-half. Tom had played alongside great players like Dimitar Berbatov, Luka Modric and Rafael Van Der Vaart. Some footballers aren't big fans like that, aren't into the history of the game as much, or chatting about past teams, discussing great players.

I'm different. I loved watching that Real Madrid team.

When Bolo signed for Sunderland, it was after he had first come to the club for a trial. He was 33 at the time. I was coming back from injury then... I remember Bolo scored a hat-trick in a training game. The gaffer asked me how I thought Bolo had done, as we were both watching the game.

Heads nodded in agreement... he could still play.

I still had a Barcelona top at the time that I wore as a kid. I loved it, the blue and red stripes, the gold writing with Rivaldo across the back. I was looking at Bolo and thinking he was part of that great Barca team... now we're teammates sharing the same dressing-room.

We were sitting at the dinner table one day in Sunderland after training. The club had signed an Argentinian defender Marcos Angeleri at the time. Myself, Marcos, Bolo and Steed were sitting in a group. Steed and Bolo were chatting away in French.

Then Marcos asked him a question and Bolo answered him in Spanish. Then I asked him something and he came back to me in English. He was comfortable moving between different languages at the same time. No problem.

He speaks fluent Dutch, German, French, Spanish and English. I found it unbelievably impressive to watch. It's one thing to say you can speak them all but another to witness someone switching freely between them and holding different conversations. It was fascinating.

I was very lucky throughout my career to be brought into contact with so many great players and great people. I don't think I fell out with too many. Of course, I came across a few bad eggs, every footballer will, but I generally tried to get along with everyone.

Not everyone I played with was a world-beater, but I played with some very good professionals. I came across lots of good characters in the Hull and Sunderland dressing-rooms.

I'm grateful to them all.

I LIKE TO look at a couple of people at the top end of every sport, studying how they go about things and carry themselves. Ronnie O'Sullivan in snooker... how he masters his craft. Tiger Woods' mentality in how he approaches golf. Sports documentaries detailing the lives of different sportspeople intrigue me.

Magic Johnson's career was phenomenal, same with Kobe Bryant and Larry Bird. Then in boxing... Lennox Lewis, hadn't realised how good he was. Got obsessed with *Drive To Survive* on Netflix and the whole world of Formula One. Fascinated by Lewis Hamilton and Max Verstappen, their rivalry in trying to win the World Championship, their contrasting characters.

I'm drawn to following the fortunes of a lot of other sportspeople, particularly the Irish ones. Shane Lowry, as I've said, is a massive Irish sports fan. I used to follow him on social media and when we were playing with Ireland, he would always send messages of encouragement, particularly when we were qualifying for the Euros in 2016, and then headed to France for the tournament and trying to qualify for the World Cup in 2018.

Then I met him in a nightclub once in Dublin. I was out with the Irish team and he came over to say hello. Just got chatting to him and kept in touch. A great fella. I'd always follow how he's doing, watch him play the Majors and the big tournaments, desperate for him to do well. To see him win The Open in 2019 in Portrush was amazing.

I think that's the way people that are involved in sport are! You want to see others from your country doing well, you're going to get behind them with your support. Katie Taylor in boxing is another example. Everybody in Ireland wants her to do so well and succeed. She's won caps as well for the Irish women's football team.

That's unbelievable, to have excelled there, then start focusing on boxing to win gold in the Olympics in London, turn professional and dominate there to become a world champion, all the while transforming her sport and increasing the popularity of it.

I admire her so much for all that.

Shane and Katie both have that down to earth quality. From knowing Shane a little, he's just a normal lad. Loves his sport, will watch whatever game or event is on that weekend on TV. I feel part of it is the gaelic games background in Ireland... Shane's dad and his uncles were very successful as gaelic footballers with Offaly. I can relate to it with all my dad has done in hurling with different county teams.

I feel having a parent involved in a sport like that gives you a strong identity. I have spent my adult life living and working and playing football in England, but the sense of belonging and link to him has never left me. Shane plays golf all around the world but you can still always see how proud he is of where he's from... Offaly, the place he grew up.

You gravitate to people like that who care about their home. Fame and money haven't changed them.

Leaving the Field

MY IRELAND CAREER petered out after the Denmark play-off in 2017. I only got three more caps afterwards, coming on as a sub in 2018 against Turkey, France and Poland.

The Polish match in Wroclaw on Tuesday September 11, 2018, was my last game for Ireland. Five days earlier we lost 4-1 to Wales in the Nations League.

I hadn't played.

We trained the next day in Cardiff. The worst session is the day after a game when you've not played. You're annoyed and if the team has got pumped, you know the coaches are going to make you work twice as hard.

My head wasn't in it at all.

Martin came up after and said, 'What the f**k is wrong with you?'

'I'm f****ng annoyed.'

'It's the worst I've ever seen you train.'

'Well, I'm pissed off we got hammered and I haven't played!'

That wasn't the main argument that got people talking.

BEFORE THE POLAND game, a voice message surfaced on social media. Stephen Ward detailing an argument Roy had with Harry Arter and Jon Walters a couple months before. It spread like wildfire.

I felt it was blown out of proportion.

I've seen Roy go mad… Martin go mad… loads of people losing the plot.

But everyone found out about this one as they listened to what Wardy had to say. The thing that most people don't know is that there was a Snapchat video recorded of the argument.

The individual had the phone on and started recording. I don't know what possessed him. I was thinking… *Jesus Christ, this can't go any further.*

Fair enough a voice-note, but not a video. The individual said it to me.

I got the phone and deleted it.

I was brought along to the pre-match Poland press conference, where Martin pointed out we'd had an argument in Cardiff and it was normal.

It happens all the time in football.

Paul McShane punched me in the changing room at half-time during a Hull game, a proper hit to the jaw. I've had more arguments with Paul than my own family… he'd fight with his own shadow in order to win. In training, if his team started losing, he'd be screaming and if you were on the other team, it was pretty funny.

That row happened on a Saturday during a defeat as Hull chased promotion at the end of the season.

Paul called me as we were going out to training on the Monday.

I just turned and said, 'Don't say what you're going to say. It's fine, move on.'

'Fair play!'

I knew Paul was so desperate to win and I was the same. Some fellas take it to heart, and I'd no grudges.

Move on. Once I get in my car to go home, it's forgotten about.

THE WALES MATCH was Wardy's last appearance for Ireland. I don't know if there was a way back for him. I know Roy rang Wardy, but there's no voice-note about that call.

Look, these things happen.

You just need to be careful in what you share with friends when you're in football. I grew more conscious of that as I got older. In the WhatsApp group of my core friends, there was an alert if I said something that wasn't to go further.

#clearchat

I didn't share everything. Any classified information I said over the years was to lads I'd trust and love, and I'd have been heartbroken if they'd shared it elsewhere. Probably wouldn't speak to them again. I built a circle of trust over years with the lads, they respected it.

I didn't think too much about that Ireland controversy. Footballers are selfish, and my concern was not playing in that Wales match. Whatever dispute exists between Roy and Jon Walters, that was their issue.

I get on really well with Jon, I get on with Roy.

Football is a small world; focus on your own relationships rather than taking sides.

Alan Pardew was linked one time with taking over as Hull manager.

How would that have played out for me? It didn't materialise but it would have been a challenge I'd have just had to face.

THE MONTH OF January 2019 was spent training with the Reading under-23s, isolated away from the football spotlight. We'd change in a Portakabin, often sharing it with the groundsmen. We were in exile; we called ourselves… 'The Bomb Squad'.

You find out who your friends are in those situations. Paul McShane and John O'Shea were brilliant, they'd come down to see us. Sam Baldock, who I'm still friends with, was in the same scenario but he was determined to outlast Gomes, which he did.

We used to joke about who would crack first. I was tipped to be last but I folded early… told the coaches I wasn't training one day and they could tear up my contract.

I was gone.

The club asked me to take time to think about it.

I rang dad on the way home; he told me to slow down and not do anything stupid. Cally was similar… she was panicking as I was being an idiot. I slept on it, went back in the next day, told Reading I was staying and told them they would pay every pound they owed me.

It started to take a toll, but then Reading brought in Seb Ewen, a transfer fixer, and it was his job to find us all clubs. He said Coventry in League One were interested in a loan move. My head was all over the place.

At Christmas, Cally and Alanna had moved back to Hull. It made sense as she was pregnant and felt more settled there; we didn't know what my future was with Reading.

Seb just asked me to speak to Mark Robins, the Coventry manager who'd famously scored that important FA Cup goal in 1990 for Man United under Alex Ferguson. Within two minutes of speaking to Mark, I had my mind made up. I joined until the end of the season, packed the car and drove up to the West Midlands. I only played five games for Coventry… injury struck again, but I loved my time at the club. Mark was great, said not to worry about my fitness and he made me feel wanted. It was a refreshing situation. A squad of young, hungry players. Michael Doyle had been at the club a long time but moved on. I was now the veteran Irish midfielder.

Mark gave me free rein to improve the squad culture.

I didn't want the mistakes of Reading repeated. The dressing-room should be a sanctuary and a place to build chemistry. I got speakers in so there'd be music on, set up a table to play Uno cards and we got players into the habit of coming in early before training.

I had no family in Coventry, so I'd stay at the ground every day until 3.30-4pm. No rush to leave. We'd do gym sessions, play cards and just hang out. The young lads would be picking my brains on training techniques, or different Premier League experiences.

We kept them disciplined… Mark would fine them for using phones in the dressing-room, I'd fine them if they were late to the gym.

The club provided me with an apartment in Coventry and then on days off I'd head home to Hull to the family. It seemed a strange existence, living on my own but I'd a nice network of players from the club… go out for dinner, watch a Champions League match or head to a pub quiz. Ways to pass the time.

My hamstring injury slowly came right. Then in April, I came on against Bristol Rovers and 13 minutes later was heading off after busting my left shoulder in a challenge for the ball. I snapped my AC joint, Grade 5. The pain was severe.

I had surgery to repair the damage and nine days later Brody was born.

I couldn't even hold him.

Cally was after a C-section and my arm was in a sling, so it was a bit chaotic in our house for those few weeks. We got a nanny in to help and we got by.

I wish I'd played more at Coventry, but I did feel I helped galvanise the squad.

It was just a shame we ran out of steam and missed the play-offs; finished eighth, but the following year they went up as champions. I had been in such a bad place at Reading, that Coventry got my buzz back for playing football.

MICK MCCARTHY CAME in as the new Ireland manager in November 2018.

I never got to play for him. We spoke on the phone a few times; he brought up that I wasn't playing much that season for Reading and Coventry. He said he needed lads playing regularly.

I fully respected that.

It didn't finish the way I wanted on the pitch with Ireland, but after I retired I was invited back to Dublin in September 2019.

Ireland played Bulgaria in a friendly and I got presented to the crowd that night with Cally, Alanna and Brody by my side. To get recognised like that was really nice. Mick was in charge during a tough, damaging time for Irish football with the constant revelations during 2019 about the finances of the FAI.

I was taken aback like everyone else by all the stories that emerged. People would ask how was I so oblivious to it all? When we met up for Ireland duty, our focus was on the pitch for training and the match that followed.

No idea what was going on in the boardrooms and offices.

I met John Delaney, the CEO, plenty of times during my Ireland career. But the interactions were always brief. He'd say well done after a game and if we made small talk, it usually revolved around hurling… how Cork and Waterford were going, or he'd ask how my dad was keeping?

As players our focus was on getting results for Ireland and that's what we cared about. At that time what John Delaney or any FAI official was doing wasn't something I was concerned about.

I came across a lot of good people in the FAI, like Peter Sherrard and Lisa Bergin, who looked after the players. The security team of Bobby, Martin and Drew. The physio Ciaran. The chef Dave. Our doctor Alan Byrne. The kitmen Dick and Mick.

To later hear all the stories that emerged about the FAI, of course it was wrong. I did get a copy of *Champagne Football*, the book that details everything. It is people in the background that suffer.

But I've spent many years in football and nothing surprises me.

MARTIN O'NEILL'S TIME with Ireland didn't end well.

There became this hostility towards him, the mood turned sour. It was tough, as I had huge time for the man. I don't think Martin helped himself at times. The interviews with RTÉ football correspondent Tony O'Donoghue made for uncomfortable viewing.

People were harping on about the unattractive football being played. Martin got results though… we qualified for the Euros and were 90 minutes away from reaching the World Cup. That was forgotten about near the finish. Didn't help that a few lads came out to put the sword in but that's football, lads who don't play always have more to say.

There's always been great pride and passion in Ireland's performances for years. I want to retain those core values and if you can add a possession-based style, that's brilliant. We can't lose the grit that makes us hard to break down.

My biggest concern for Stephen Kenny when he took over, was when would he get that opportunity to work on an expansive style of football? International windows are narrow; it's difficult to implement something complex.

Stephen has done brilliantly in bringing through young players, but getting results is not easy. Martin was able to dig out games. The day Martin left Ireland, I had finished training with Reading when someone told me the news.

Rather than text him, I'd more respect and rang him. We spoke on the phone for an hour as I drove home, reminiscing about different times.

I chatted with Roy later; I knew he didn't want sympathy then. But I felt it was right to talk to Martin. He was the manager when I'd had my best moments for Ireland.

I can't say a bad word about him.

My career in the English game ended with Reading (left) and Coventry City.

I had different experiences at the end of my career, bad with Reading, good with Coventry, but that career came to a sudden halt because of my ongoing injuries. I am lucky to be able to reflect however (as Roy Keane reminded me) on a memorable career in the Premier League and celebrating a few goals along the way.

GAMING

IN THOSE FIRST few years after moving to England, I acted like an idiot at times. You're a professional footballer, you get excited... you become too big for your boots.

I was young and earning too much money.

Coming back to Cork, I'd go out and pay for all my buddies. If I wanted to go on holidays and the lads couldn't afford it, I'd pay and then they'd have no excuse for not going. I had a brilliant upbringing from great parents but the money and fame made me get a bit ahead of myself.

When I was 19, there were three cars I really liked.

An Audi A3.

A classic BMW M3.

And an Mk2 Golf GTi.

I couldn't decide which one I wanted, so I ended up buying them all. I've no idea what I was thinking. Eventually I was just looking at the three in the garage.

Dad asked me what the thinking was in owning three cars? As he rightly pointed out, I could only drive one at a time. I sold two of them quick enough.

I had some fantastic times as well.

The summer of 2013 started by going to Marbella straight after we got promoted with Hull. I came home, went out in Leeds that night... next day flew to Ibiza. Back for two days, then a trip to New York and Las Vegas. Finished off with time at home in Cork and then back for pre-season.

Different lads came for different trips... Kelogs was there for them all. A brilliant, mad couple of months. We were young, no responsibilities and living the dream. It took me a while to figure out this way of life. I wouldn't say I thought I was better than people, but I got drawn into arguments, especially back home in Cork when there was drink involved. Looking back, I think I needed those experiences; they served as a wake-up call and I matured. And ultimately, what 23-year-old wouldn't be affected by earning tens of thousands of pounds a week?

WHEN I STARTED playing for Hull, we'd get a few kids coming up after games for autographs and pictures. After a couple of years, the crowd had grown to 100. The increase wasn't to do with my performances for Hull, it was all to do with video gaming and *Fifa*.

My dad would be looking on and trying to get his head around it.

I was always into video games growing up like everyone else. Around 2015, I got really into *Fifa* and one of the lads suggested I should start online streams when I played. Then a young fella asked me could I upload the streams to YouTube, so he could watch them back as he had missed one.

I looked into it, set up my own YouTube channel and it became a hobby.

It's grown to over 340,000 subscribers, people watching on when I play. It's something I enjoy. When I played football, the *Fifa* gaming was a way to switch off.

It was never a problem when I played for Hull, but at Reading there was a perception I was more interested in video gaming than being a footballer. Fans had a pop off me over it but it honestly never affected my performances.

It helped me relax.

I'd play in a hotel room before Ireland games or the big matches with Hull. My biggest downfall was I publicised the fact I was gaming, but loads of footballers do it, bringing a PlayStation or an Xbox with them for away trips. It's a way to unwind and kill time. Apparently, Martin and Roy were intrigued about the YouTube videos, so they watched them one day.

'Ah, they're very good David!' said Martin.

Not sure if they later became subscribers.

People tune into the streams for the personality of the gamer and the content, how good they are at it. Esports is a different world but it's growing massively. Look at Logan Paul... he started uploading videos and ended up fighting Floyd Mayweather.

On the outside it may seem strange but there is an enormous market for the industry. When I retired, people assumed I might go at it full-time. But you would have to devote all your time and the big money if you're professional is in other games like *Fortnite* or *CS:GO.*

Gaming is a hobby, something to play online with my friends when we all catch up and have a few drinks on a Friday night.

I'D BE CONSCIOUS that I put my body through a lot of stress for 13, 14 years. That's why I had to retire and when I did... my body needed a break.

One of my strengths as a footballer was my endurance. I was able to keep running and I took pride in that. At times like the hard pre-season work, I wanted to beat people and I wanted to see them struggling because I wanted them to know I was better runner than them, that I was fitter than them.

My lifestyle is far different now.

Laziness has probably crept in, and I'm naturally not in the shape I was. I don't believe it's difficult to get it back, you can find a way to incorporate fitness work into your daily life.

When dad comes over to visit us in Hull, he brings his bike. He'll head out in the morning and I'll often go with him. At home he cycles regularly, doing a 30km loop, three to four times a week. He travels at his own pace.

Someone asked him once when he was on the bike over here in England, was he on Strava? He said, 'No I'm just on the bike'.

He's not fussed about what time anyone else is doing, his focus is just on him cycling. Dad is in his mid-sixties, he still is a fit man.. it's an example of a trait that I've admired more in him as I've got older.

Golf is something I got into after retiring.

I'm a member of a club in Cottingham. I would like to play more often because I'd like to get really good. Then it's in my mind... *I'm trying to improve for what? To compete competitively?*

I enjoy playing it but the way I'm wired when it comes to sport is... *what can I get out of it?* As a 33-year-old, I'd wonder what height I could get to? I think that comes from having played sport professionally, it's all about striving to reach the next level.

I look at the story of JR Smith.

An American basketball player, he won two NBA titles, one with the Cleveland Cavaliers in 2016 and the other with the LA Lakers in 2020. Then the following year his life went in a different direction, he went back to college in North Carolina and joined their golf team, which is an elite standard. That intrigues me. A guy who has achieved so much in one sport and now he's trying to do something in another one.

So that's sort of how I view golf.

If I'm going to dedicate a lot of time to it, what am I going to get out of it or will it just become a hobby?

I often played rounds of golf after I retired with Gaz Beadle. People would know him from being on the reality TV series *Geordie Shore*. I got to know him simply from going out in Newcastle when I played for Sunderland. He's a year older than me. At the time they were obviously flavour of the week as the TV show was so popular. We were footballers, had something similar in terms of recognition in public.

I got to know quite a few of them.

His life has gone 180 degrees in last few years. For a long time it was all about being out every night of the week, making nightclub appearances, operating in the public eye. Now he's a family man. He lives about an hour north of Hull.

We were chatting one day and he was talking about golf. I mentioned I played and he just said we need to play a round together. So it went from there. His kids were in nursery three days a week, and that was his green light to play golf those mornings. Same story for me, once Brody started nursery... then both the kids were out in the mornings.

It fitted perfectly. I'd head up to near him and we'd play a course nearby, then the next day he'd drive down and we'd go around Cottingham. It was really enjoyable. Someone who's good fun to play with.

We'd have a fifty quid prize for the winner, put a bit of competition into it, get us both going. A nice way to spend a morning in the spring and summer months.

My Home

I STILL KEEP a close eye on how Hull are doing.

2022 felt like a time of huge transition for the club. A new owner arrived in Acun Ilıcalı and a new manager was appointed in Shota Arveladze. That means the club is heading in a new direction.

The previous owner Assem Allam was fantastic to me and my family. His time in charge turned very sour though with the controversy over the name change. The attendances dropped, a lot of people were left very disgruntled.

I found there was a lot of good people still in the club trying their best to make things change but it just wasn't happening and having an impact. The sale of the club in early 2022 brought an injection of life that was probably needed.

It's just a different atmosphere now, but I'll still go to the stadium and watch games. That passion for football is still there in the area. Obviously, with two rugby league clubs in the city, Hull FC are traditionally supported by those in the west side and Hull Kingston Rovers are supported by the east side.

Hull FC share the MKM Stadium with Hull City. Those rugby league sides do take up a large proportion of sports fans in the city.

I think with the football club around 2015-16, the divide between the fans and the ownership really took hold. You compare the support we had following us in 2014 for the FA Cup run, with two games at Wembley, to the 2016 play-off final when we headed to London. The difference was really noticeable. A lot of fans refused to go to home games for a few years. It was sad to see a situation like that develop but, thankfully, that has gradually started to change for the better.

I would never say the passion and interest in the football club were diluted, there was just a lot of frustration at how things were being run and how situations were being handled. In that climate, fans weren't as willing to part with their money for tickets to games. It would be unfair of me to suggest the fans stopped supporting the team. They were more cheering on from a distance than being consistently present in the matchday crowd.

The sense of support had changed but it was still there.

THE SCENE AT Hull has changed a lot from my playing days.

The last Hull City player in action that I'd shared a dressing-room with was George Honeyman and that link was from our Sunderland days. George was a young fella making his way at the Stadium of Light when I was in the first team. He's since moved on to Millwall.

In my last year at Hull, there was a huge turnover of players and that relentless cycle of change continued. There's still a Cork link on the playing side with the defender Sean McLoughlin.

I've only ever met Sean a couple of times in passing. I've watched him from afar because you'd always take an interest in footballers from Ireland, especially one that played for Hull and came from Cork City. I wouldn't have gone out of my way to introduce myself or anything like that. You have to respect the fact that you're retired and not involved in the club any more.

My relationship with Brian Lenihan, for example, was totally different, a young player who joined from Cork City in 2014 when I was still playing for the club.

It's nice though to see another Cork link with Hull City and the team are back in the Championship. Sean moved over to England a little bit older than I did; he went on loan to St Mirren in Scotland and did well there, before coming back to Hull and really settling into a defensive role

I'M ALWAYS INTERESTED in following guys that I played with and watching how their careers have developed. Jarrod Bowen is seven years younger than me; my final season with Hull in 2017-18 was the time where his career really started to take off. He made a few appearances in the Premier League when we got relegated in 2017 but then exploded to life in the Championship. A regular in our team and a really important goalscorer. By the end of the season he won all the club Player of the Year awards. He was incredible.

In my early years at Hull, I used to go watch the reserve side when they were playing on a Tuesday night. I didn't have the kids at the time… it was an enjoyable way to pass an evening. I remember Jarrod playing.

He always intrigued me because he always seemed to be in the right place at the right time for that tap-in close to goal, or had this ability to manoeuvre the space to get a shot off. You looked at him doing it at that level on a consistent basis. It was impressive.

Then the question was could he do it with the first team?

He soon proved he could do so. His career has been on this upward trajectory for a long time. When he broke into the Hull first team, he hit 14 league goals that first season, then 22 the year after, and 16 in the season after that. Numbers like that get you noticed.

By January 2020, West Ham came calling and got the cheque book out. You could see his impact on that Hull group. They were never the same that season after he left and by July were relegated from the Championship.

Jarrod has kept rising in his career, scoring in the Premier League and making his debut for England. Every time it has been required to reach a higher level, Jarrod has achieved it. That beautiful knack of appearing on the end of crosses is still there, similar to Raheem Sterling's ability in that way.

That combination of pace, positioning and anticipation gets you into those positions. Jarrod's always had a terrific work ethic as well, and the West Ham players and David Moyes speak about that. A good kid, very professional.

I FEEL VERY fortunate to still have such a link to Hull City. I spent a large chunk of my playing career here.

I do have a real connection with the place.

It's great.

I have good relationships with so many people working here and they're so good to me. Being able to bring my kids down to the pitch to meet the Hull mascots, I appreciate that I'm still in a position to do things like that.

It is a homely club in a way, it has retained that community vibe. There was that divide between the fanbase and the club but it has been bridged and repaired. Joe Clutterbrook deserves so much credit for that. He's the club's chief commercial officer and has done incredible work at bringing people together.

When I retired from football in 2019, and I was gone from Hull for a while at that stage, it was Joe who rang to invite me and the family to a home game where I was presented on the pitch to the fans. Joe has fought tooth and nail to solve some of the fans' issues with tickets, introducing different ventures. A lot of people within the club will give him the credit but people outside won't know the work he does in driving everything.

I can see the connection between the fans and the club has slowly but surely come back, now it's about regaining stability. The drop to League One was a huge disappointment, that slide from the top tier in the space of a few years... but they got promoted in the spring of 2021 and are finding their feet in the Championship now.

It takes time.

You can't shoot for the moon straightaway.

I feel the Hull City teams I played in and the moments we produced for the club will be remembered forever.

The trips to Wembley.

The FA Cup run.

The club has only been promoted to the Premier League three times and I was involved twice. I hope to see them get back to the top level of English football again and when they do, I'll be there still cheering on Hull City.

WHEN I RETIRED, we were initially thinking of moving to Manchester... Didsbury is just south of the city centre, that's where Cally is from. We looked all over the city, but especially around there. Couldn't really find something we liked, we would have had to downgrade the house as to get something similar was going to cost a lot more. I'd just retired and was conscious of putting a lot of money into something that I wasn't sure we needed.

We talked about building a house, maybe going back to Ireland to do that.

Cally had no interest in moving to Cork, with her family in Manchester. I left home at 18 so it made no difference to me, it's become like second nature to be away. My sister was the same… she went away to college in Limerick at 18 and got a job in Wexford after that. My dad talks about both of us being gone at a young age.

So Cally was happy to stay around Hull and so was I. Ultimately that was the best place for us to settle.

Will I go back to Ireland?

I bounce this topic back and forth with dad. I have ambitions to get into coaching and management. Going down the road of returning to Ireland, the aim would be ultimately to get back to England. There are more potential opportunities here, more clubs and teams nearby.

Will Hull be the base for the rest of my life?

Who knows? I'm not sure will we stay here forever. Things might change when the kids grow older. But for right now, it is a great place to live and we are very happy here.

I'm the only one of the core playing group I was part of who is still living in Hull. During my first few years here, the majority of our team lived in Hull. From 2015 on we had players settled in different areas travelling to Hull and then more moved on in the last stint of their careers, setting up base where they wanted to be when they retire.

It's all understandable, as there was links drawing players to a variety of areas. I always thought that I would move back to Cork, but for me, a loan move for a few months has turned into a decade of living here. When I first joined Hull, the club got me an apartment but I still held onto my house in Sunderland, and I'd go up there on days off.

But then I bought the house in Cottingham and later we just got settled as a family. My wife loves the place, my kids are happy in school. It's a case of why would I move? I like the area and the people, it reminds me of Cork in both respects.

I'd never have thought I'd still be living here a decade later.

My dream was always to move home. It's a funny dilemma that faces Irish players. Of those I played with that I'd be close to from our international days, I think James McClean is the only one guaranteed to move home. James is a month older than me, we were both born in 1989. I think he has a target still to play for Derry City.

Seamus Coleman is settled in Liverpool a long time now, playing with Everton. His wife is from Killybegs as well, but they have three kids and have put down roots where they are. Family circumstances change plans, especially when the kids get settled. I see that with my own, Alanna and Brody.

Now that Alanna has started school, you don't want to be uprooting and moving.

Myself and Cally have talked about the coaching ambitions I want to pursue. We feel that even if I got a job somewhere else around the country, although ideally it'd be somewhere close to Yorkshire, that Cally and the kids would stay in Cottingham. We're within a two hour drive of a lot of places from here.

It's home.

Cally and myself celebrate our wedding with family and friends, and most of all, our daughter Alanna (top).

It was a memorable journey for me and my family, and I got to say my farewell to Irish fans in September 2019 at the Aviva Stadium, when I had Brody and Allana for company. A brilliant experience.

The Game

THEY SAY EVERY professional athlete has two lives.

One ends when you retire and the other ends when you die. I retired in August 2019, and even a few years on it was really surreal that I was no longer... *David Meyler the footballer.*

I had started studying for my coaching badges just before I retired but didn't have any definite coaching plan mapped out in my mind at that stage.

What do I want to do?

Initially, the lack of routine after I retired was hard to deal with. Football had come first for so long... and everything else worked around that.

I needed direction, and I was lucky that I got two phone calls.

One was for a job interview for *Uncut*, a series the Premier League filmed, and they asked me down to London to screen test for a presenting role. It went well and I got the position to interview Premier League players.

The second was from my old Cork City teammate Colin O'Brien, who was now the head coach of the Ireland under-17 team.

We had a general conversation about my career. He was asking to see how was I doing in coming to terms with my playing days coming to an end. Then he wanted to know was I interested in getting involved in coaching the Ireland under-17s.

Colin knew me from a young age at Cork City and also that I was completing my UEFA A licence at the time. Maybe he felt I was a right match for his coaching team. I'm still there anyway, so I must be doing something right.

My title is technical coach. The label is just a fancy title really. I'm just a coach. Colin is our head coach, the buck stops with him. We're all there to assist them, we're given responsibilities to take on and they must be delivered to the standard he wants.

I'm getting better at that but I am a young, inexperienced coach. I may have played the game at a high level but understanding football and being able to teach that to others are two completely different things.

It is challenging.

I know from my own days playing for Ireland that your time with the players is limited. The amount of detail and work that is done behind the scenes to make sure those few days run smoothly is just phenomenal. If we've a meeting with the players at 5pm, we as a coaching team will have had lunch and then spent couple hours sitting down together to plan that meeting… go through the purpose of it, have all our video clips ready of ourselves or opposition to show the players.

Hours are spent debating how best to get the message across in a 15-20 minute window. I never realised as a player with Ireland or at club level with Hull or Sunderland, how much effort and detail went into planning to allow the players to perform.

IT'S BEEN A great journey working with the Ireland under-17 team. In that respect it was such a shame Covid hit when it did in early 2020, as I was really starting to get into the flow of working with them.

You dip your toes into it, start to build relationships with some really good young players, share your ideas on the game and see signs of development. We were just finished a trip to Spain to play Switzerland and then our schedule was ripped up, and we were looking at each other on screens for months with countless meetings on Zoom.

It was a pity, but Covid impacted so many plans.

After I retired I was hoping to increase my coaching knowledge by visiting Premier League clubs and observing training sessions with a view to gaining an insight into how other managers worked. I wanted to upskill and see what coaching methods were being used. Playing at a high level of the game for so long meant I had plenty of contacts.

In the spring of 2020, I had set up time for myself to go watch Liverpool, Leeds United and Leicester City up close. Watching how managers like Jurgen Klopp, Marcelo Bielsa and Brendan Rodgers operated would have been fascinating. But once the pandemic hit, football had to shut down like everything else in the world and even when games returned, it was no longer possible to go in person to watch teams train.

It's a regret I didn't get that chance at the time, but I've just had to adapt.

Life presents different opportunities. I got introduced in 2022 to a lady who runs football academies. It came about through a mutual friend, a lad who used to work with Hull and now works with Leeds. The company is based in Huddersfield with the academies around Yorkshire. Leeds United defender Liam Cooper and Manchester City midfielder Kalvin Phillips both have academies.

So it took off from there and the DM7 Football Academy was born.

We set it up in Bishop Burton in Beverley, just a 20 minute drive north of Hull. It's run for under-4 to under-14... all the academies have about 300 kids. We got it off the ground in June. It takes place in Friday evenings. Divide the pitch into eight sections, have 12 kids working the football in each section for an hour.

Then another group of kids come in after they're finished.

My role is to sort of oversee it all. The company select the coaches, who all have to meet certain criteria and follow a 12-week programme which ensures an individual plan for each kid. I was blown away from the first meeting with the amount of detail laid out. It's really well structured, they've been doing it now for eight years and by now really have the running of it nailed down.

IN OCTOBER 2021, we at last got to play games and test ourselves with the Republic of Ireland under-17 team. The qualifying began for the 2022 UEFA Under-17 Championships in Israel. Our first round of qualifying took place back home in Cork over the space of a week... we beat Andorra and North Macedonia before drawing with Poland.

In March 2022, we headed to Portugal for three games in the elite round of qualifying, which would determine if we were going to get the prize of tournament football that we wanted. We lost 4-1 in the opener against Portugal. A bad start. Things didn't improve with a defeat to Finland and a draw against Bulgaria.

We had so many hopes and expectations for the games and then it all didn't go to plan for various different reasons. I got Covid the week before we were due to travel. I wasn't feeling well one afternoon… tight chest and coughing, tested myself and was positive. Isolated away from Cally and the kids for couple days in the office I built for myself in our shed during lockdown.

They'd leave meals for me at the door or I'd chat away to the kids. The timing was really disappointing. I felt my own preparations for the tournament were impacted, I was late joining the rest of the squad and coaching team.

Our second game was against Finland, they were the team I was designated to study. I watched hours of footage of games Finland had played in. Then I had regular Zoom calls with the rest of the coaching team, trying to give them a sense of how Finland played… this is how they press, these are their strengths… pinpointing any small detail that could make a difference.

We played Belgium in a warm-up match previously and got chatting to the Belgian staff after. They mentioned they'd a game upcoming against Finland, so I flew over to Brussels to watch. Headed over that morning, stayed the night and back the following day. It was a brief trip and I remember sitting in the airport on the way home thinking that this is what my dad did for me throughout my career… going over to all those Hull and Sunderland games to support me.

Fly over, watch the game, fly back home.

When the opportunity first came for me to work with the Ireland team, dad pointed out that this was why I'd worked to get my coaching licence in the first place. It was time to go down that road and see how I found it.

It's been good for me, a gateway into what the coaching world entailed. We work in the international windows during the club season, playing games and going on training camps. All it has done is make me hungrier to go into full-time coaching.

That's the ultimate aim.

I want to stay involved in football and getting to work with Colin O'Brien and the Irish under-17s has been a brilliant experience for me, for which I am so grateful. Hopefully it is the start of a long career in the game on the other side of the sideline.

THANK YOU

WHEN I DAMAGED my shoulder in April 2019, I was facing 12-to-16 weeks out. I saw it as a prime opportunity to rest my right knee and get ready for pre-season. Coventry were good at helping, but I ended up finishing my rehab at home and hired my own physio, Stuart Leake who'd been with Hull City before.

But the lack of exercise saw my knee deteriorate. It faded away.

The clock was ticking.

As that summer progressed, I started doing some running but my knee was in so much pain. My physio recommended seeing a surgeon in Leeds in June and he sketched out the three options.

1. Tidy up the knee with a minor procedure, get four or five weeks relief, but soon you'll be back to square one.
2. Drill four holes in my kneecap on either side, to relieve pressure. A very specialised surgery costing £50-60k. A 10-15 percent chance of getting back playing and it would require at least 18 months rehab. I needed to fund all that myself.
3. Call it a day.

Take your pick.

There was talk of a knee replacement. I was 30. The shock of that was like getting a punch to the jaw.

I left Leeds that day, and rang dad and Cally. I think my family felt it was all in my head at times, but I knew how much pain I was in. Even now my knee is riddled with arthritis and on a cold morning when I wake up, it is painful as I walk down the stairs.

The decision weighed on my mind over the coming weeks.

There was an obvious choice to make, but I couldn't bring myself to say those words... *I'm going to have to retire from football*. Part of me refused to accept it.

I was only 30... if I'd got to 35 I'd have been content.

I had to sort out my Reading situation. Even if I wasn't playing, my contract wasn't up. I'd started to make peace with the fact that I was going to retire but it was about my children now and I wanted to get paid.

My agent was clever; he'd put a contract clause in that if I was fit for a certain number of games, I got an extra year. Dad had written down every game I was available for, including when I was at Coventry, as that was Reading's choice not to select me. I did some of the negotiations myself. Mark Bowen, a former Welsh player, was handling it for Reading.

It was a game of poker.

We eventually struck a deal. I got paid 70 percent of what I was owed and moved on. Soccer began as a sport for me. Later, I realised it was a job in a cut-throat industry and, by the end, it was a ruthless business where everyone had to look out for themselves.

I WAS 30 when I retired, entitled to feel my football career had been cut short sooner than it should have. My wife and my father always thought I was going to have a breakdown at some stage.

I kept watching games, went to the Champions League final in Madrid to see Jordan lift the trophy, saw my former teammates in action and did punditry work.

It was as if they feared all that exposure to football would overwhelm me.

Gradually, I just learned to make peace with it though. I'm happy for all the lads still playing. This is their moment.

I had my mine.

I did what I set out to do as a kid and I'm thankful for that.

ROY KEANE PUT it best, when he rang me after I retired.

'Don't look back with regrets.

'Look at what you've achieved.

'You've had an incredible career.'

I was taken aback by him saying that. It doesn't stack up at all next to his. But he put it into perspective... that medals and trophies are not the only measure. Football is so competitive and so global, that for an Irish player to make it for a time in the Premier League is a real achievement.

ON WEDNESDAY JULY 31, 2019, it was officially announced that my contract with Reading had been terminated by mutual consent. By coincidence it was the same afternoon that dad left his position as Cork senior hurling manager.

A day of departures for the family.

The decision on my future was dragging on. On Friday August 30, I put it up on Instagram and let the whole world know... I was retiring.

The picture I chose for that post was from that night in Cardiff in 2017, when I grabbed the crest on the white Ireland jersey and felt that rush of joy from succeeding with my country.

At the end of the statement, I paid tribute to Cally, dad, mum and Sarah for their support. The final two lines summed up the journey.

You've helped a young boy live out his dreams.

Thank you for everything.

EPILOGUE

· · · · · · · · · ·

Sarah Meyler

SPORT WAS ALWAYS huge in our family.

As kids, we were always going to matches, and so much of what we did revolved around sport. Mom and dad never pushed us into anything, they wanted us to do well and gave us every opportunity. I was big into swimming… that was mom's background.

David couldn't handle the early mornings for the pool, he liked his sleep.

There was never a problem with our parents in getting up early to take me to the pool, or driving David to training or a match. When I went to college in Limerick, to Mary Immaculate to study teaching, I was trying to keep swimming going in the 50-metre pool in UL.

I'd swam for Ireland when I was younger and to a high level, but it just wasn't working for me. I gave it up in the end and when I told mom and dad, they were so supportive.

They'd always back our decisions.

· · · · · · · · · ·

Peter 'Kelogs' Kelleher

DAVID AND MYSELF grew up 100 metres from each other. I'm from Lissadell and he's Rochestown Rise in Cork, a short walkway between the two estates.

From the age of six, we just became best friends.

Dave was the fella that was talented at every sport. We'd play soccer constantly on the green, or spend summers in Douglas Golf Club as we got older. He was big into GAA; I always thought he was a brilliant hurler.

We'd slag him when he was younger… 'You'll go off to soccer trials in England and come back with a Dublin accent from hanging out with those lads'.

•••••••••

Sarah

WHATEVER SPORTING ROAD David went down, he'd have excelled at it.

He has such a driven mentality.

When he dropped out of school, I thought at first it was ridiculous but the opinion of his older sister wasn't going to matter.

When he moved to England, he vowed he would make it. When he tore his cruciate, he vowed to get back.

If he puts his mind to something, he'll achieve it. He wasn't the flashiest footballer; he was a workhorse and would do whatever a manager asked him to do for the team.

David's core group of friends always stayed supporting him. They'd all travel to games and I thought that was a special part of it… seeing them all at the FA Cup final with Hull jerseys and Meyler written on the back. Kelogs was constantly heading over to him… he's like the fifth member of our family, and always there for David.

Dad put so much time into travelling the length and breadth of England. I don't know how he did it. It was great for David to have him there.

•••••••••

Kelogs

WE WENT TO different schools in Cork city. I went to Presentation Brothers College and he went to Christians Brothers College, a 20-minute walk between them either side of the River Lee.

Rugby was the big sport in both. In 2007, I was playing as a prop in the front row when Pres won the Munster Senior Cup… and Dave was the Christians cheerleader in the stand. We were both so into sport growing up. I was playing rugby to a high level… Munster and Ireland under-18s. Dave was excelling at everything.

I played for Cork Con in the All-Ireland league for a few years, went to Newcastle in Australia to play for a year, came back to play a bit in Cork, and then in Dublin when I moved there for work. Dave was a great supporter.

He'd come to games with John when I was in Cork. I'd a Fiat Stilo car at the time. Dave used to borrow it if he was home at weekends. The other rugby lads reckoned he was the only Premier League player driving around in a Fiat.

He'd always return it with a tank full of petrol.

* * * * * * * * *

Sarah

WHEN DAVID WAS playing for Hull, if fans were abusing him, there were times I'd shout back. One man at a Hull kept on giving out and calling him… 'Mailer'.

I turned around.

'If you're going to make fun of him, at least say his name right.'

Mom was similar. There was an Ireland game where a fella kept on saying how bad Ireland were and she just asked… 'Why did you bother paying for the ticket?'

* * * * * * * * *

Kelogs

HE WAS SO driven in everything he did. We used to play *Rugby 06* on the PlayStation… I was better than him. His grandmother then bought him the game. I didn't see him for weeks, and then called down to his house one day and he started hammering me. So competitive… such a hard worker.

That's why he got so far in England and was able to bounce back from injuries. I never doubted him. I went over a lot to him after he got injured… I was in college and had plenty of spare time. He was working hard in rehab but it was tough for him.

Joining Sunderland was a big deal for all of us. The first summer he drove home in a lovely new Audi A5, and we were all like… 'He's actually made it!'

I went over to a lot of games; the big highlights were following him at Hull. I was at the Hull-Cardiff game with John that decided promotion in 2013… and Dave jumped into the stand with us after the game.

The two of them bawling in each other's arms. It was a class moment.

• • • • • • • • •

Sarah

I FOUND PARTS of the Cork job hard when dad was in charge as manager.

Part of the problem was I'd read social media… some of the stuff was horrible, same when David was playing with Ireland. The two of them would be giving out to me… telling me not to read it. It all affected me more than the two of them.

But we had some great days. The Munster final win in 2018 with Cork was magical. And myself, mom and dad had a brilliant time following Ireland around France for Euro 2016.

It's funny, sport provided days when the four of us could be together. On Christmas Day we mightn't all be in the one place. Mom could be working; she'd be in Ireland with me. Then David and dad could be in England.

But matches were occasions to all be present.

When dad won the Cork title as manager of the Courcey Rovers club in 2011, we were all there as David was home. We got a photo after the match in Páirc Uí Rinn… David has it blown up and on the wall in his house in England.

• • • • • • • • •

Kelogs

OFTEN, WE WENT to support Dave as a group… the seven or eight lads from Cork. The Denmark play-off… and Hull's FA Cup final in 2014 were unreal occasions. When the team lost, we tried to be there for him… take him out for a few drinks.

Ask any of our buddies, and they'll all say Dave is extremely generous. He was on good money through soccer but he always wanted to look after us… just enjoy himself with his friends.

Dave hangs out with the exact same crew now that he did when we were all teenagers. He hasn't lost touch.

. . . .

Sarah

LOOKING BACK, I probably wish I went over to see David play more. Those were trips that were amazing when David played… or scored. The other side was if he wasn't playing or the club had signed another midfielder… that'd be a challenge to face.

The Ireland games were huge experiences.

We'd have the wait to hear the team named before the game to find out if he was starting. If David was a sub, I'd be more interested in watching the sideline to see if Martin O'Neill was going to call him at any stage.

The Wales game in Cardiff was the best night. Myself, mom, dad and my partner Eugene were all there; it was fantastic from start to finish. It was the first away Ireland match I was at. Walking across the car park before with mom to get a cup of coffee, and hearing he was in the team… so exciting.

. . . .

Kelogs

I WAS VERY lucky… he included me in a lot of amazing experiences. He got invited to Steven Gerrard's Golf Classic in the Algarve. We flew out and played golf the day before. We were about to tee off and four lads came down at the same time.

Meyler is saying hello… we all shake hands. I whispered to Meyler… 'Who are they?'

'That's Gerrard and his buddies.'

'What?!'

I didn't recognise Gerrard at all… he was smaller in real life than I thought he'd be.

Before I hit my drive, Gerrard shouts out in his Scouse accent… 'Right big lad… let's see what you've got!'

• • • • • • • • •

Sarah

WHEN DAVID WALKED out before a match, I'd nearly well up… nearly praying that that game would go well for my younger brother. You'd want the team to win, but I almost wanted David to play well first. Maybe that was because I was aware of the criticism if he didn't have a good game.

I think it's remarkable what he achieved given his injuries. He had to battle back on his own, motivate himself and stick at it to recover. That's something in his character that a lot of people don't have… an ability to never stop.

• • • • • • • • •

Kelogs

I'D A RUGBY match with Cork Con on a Saturday, but David was home and headed out on the Friday night. He texted me at 11.30pm.

'Any chance of a lift home?'

'Ah no, Dave. I've a game tomorrow.'

'I'm just out with Roy here.'

'Oh right… yeah I'm on my way.'

So that was the first time I met Roy Keane. Any fella in Cork would drop what they're doing to pick him up.

I met Roy a few times after that. In 2014, Ireland were playing Portugal in New York… Dave told me to come over, we were going on holidays after. I got a taxi to the team hotel and was waiting in the lobby for him.

Roy walked into the hotel and sort of did a double take when he saw me. I wasn't going to bother him, but he came back 10 minutes later… asked was I alright waiting, to go to the bar or reception if I needed anything. Very sound of him.

All those Irish lads that I got to know were good fellas. At one Ireland camp, Daryl Murphy asked Dave, 'Is Kelogs coming to the game tomorrow night?'

Then someone else shouted, 'Oh yeah… how is Kelogs?'

Roy was listening in.

'How does everybody know this Coco Pops fella?!'

• • • • • • • • • •

Sarah

IT'S FUNNY THE way it's worked out, that I'm settled in Wexford now… not too far from where dad grew up. I live in Ballymitty and work in Wexford Town… principal of St Iberius NS.

Dad comes down regularly, goes for a swim nearby and comes in for a coffee after. He's just a great help with everything… when I was building my house, or if I needed help in school.

I went all over the country to watch matches when he was a manager, just my way of supporting him.

Sport made dad and David well known.

When I started working in the school where I am now, the kids there didn't know that I was David's sister. The chat started one day about the Premier League… and I mentioned that my brother had played in it.

'Stop Ms Meyler… your brother did not play soccer!'

'He did… Google it now when you go home!'

They came in the next day; they couldn't believe it and just wanted to hear stories about David's soccer career.

• • • • • • • • • •

Kelogs

HIS FAMILY WERE central to it in driving Dave… his dad in particular. Dave idolised John when he was growing up, and what he'd achieved in sport.

And we're all very proud of Dave with everything he has now achieved.

Watching the two of them, best friends… it's what every father and son would wish for!

Printed in Great Britain
by Amazon

13969565R00135